From Images to Thinking

Waldorf Journal Project #17

Compiled and edited by
DAVID MITCHELL

> Happiness is a butterfly which, when pursued,
> is always just beyond your grasp, but which,
> if you will sit down quietly, may alight upon you.
>
> – Nathaniel Hawthorne

Printed with support from the Waldorf Curriculum Fund

Published by:

Waldorf Publications at the
Research Institute for Waldorf Education
38 Main Street
Chatham, NY 12037

Waldorf Journal Project #17
Title: *From Images to Thinking*
Editor: David Mitchell
Translators: Helen Fox, Brigitte Knaack, Nina Kuettel,
   Margot M. Saar, Ted Warren
Layout: Ann Erwin
© 2011 by AWSNA Publications, reprinted 2015
ISBN #9781-936367-71-9

Note: The Rudolf Steiner Bookstore has published a booklet of Eileen Hutchins' lectures entitled *Observation, Thinking, the Senses.*

Contents

5   Foreword

7   Children Learn in Images
Rosemary Wermbter

11   The Fairy Tale of the Crystal Ball
Christianne Brown

30   Interpreting Fairy Tales
Rudolf Steiner

51   How to Create, Tell, and Recall a Story
Rudolf Steiner

56   The Secret of Children's Pictures
Armin Krenz

61   Research into Resilience
Christof Wiechert

66   Resilient Children: First Food or Fast Food
Katherine Train

69   Why Waldorf Works: From a Neuroscientific Perspective
Regalena Melrose, MD

75   The Senses
Eileen M. Hutchins

80   The Training of Observation
Eileen M. Hutchins

Contents

83   Observation and Thinking
         Eileen M. Hutchins

89   The Activity of Thinking
         Eileen M. Hutchins

103 An Education for Our Time
         Christof Wiechert

120 A Bold Step Forward
         Andreas Neider

125 Internet Crutch
         Mathias Maurer

Foreword

The *Waldorf Journal Project,* sponsored by the Waldorf Curriculum Fund, brings translations of essays, magazine articles, and specialized studies from around the world to English-speaking audiences. This seventeenth edition begins with an essay about how children learn in images and then follows with articles about fairy tales and stories, and how a teacher can present them to the children.

Other essays discuss the resilience demonstrated by children and how children benefit from Waldorf education from a neuroscientific study as viewed by a medical doctor. Several essays from Eileen Hutchins follow addressing the senses, how observation can be quickened, and how this pertains to thinking. The final three chapters are contemporary essays about our modern life.

We hope that this *Journal* will help teachers and others gain insight into the seeds of Waldorf education. For those not interested in downloading the material, spiral bound copies are available from:

Waldorf Publications
38 Main Street
Chatham, NY 12037

by phone at: 518/634-2222
or by e-mail at: robin@waldorf-research.org

The editor, David Mitchell, was interested in receiving your comments on the material for this publication during his lifetime. We at Waldorf Publications are interested, in the spirit of his limitless interest in research from the field and in the news, in hearing from you. We would also be interested in hearing what areas you would like to see represented in future *Journal* projects. If you know of specific articles that you would like to see translated, please contact Waldorf Publications.

– The Editorial Staff
Waldorf Journal Projects

Children Learn in Images
Why Waldorf Schools Put so Much Emphasis on the Concrete

by Rosemarie Wermbter
translated by Nina Kuettel

"Can God make a rock that is so heavy that He can't lift it?" This difficult question was asked by a five-and-a-half year old boy. He had come into the "philosophical age" shortly before formal schooling, and had begun to question the world with many "whys."

Preschool age children do not have any abstract concepts available to them for philosophical questions. In their place, a concrete picture arises. Reality must be perceivable. If a mother says something like, "If he doesn't come soon, I'll see red," the child will look around for something red. A child will listen to the same short fairy tale over and over again because he always experiences it as something new. He lives in the present.

A year later, he is standing before a tree. Suddenly, he closes his eyes and, after a while, proudly announces: "I can still see the tree." Or, another time: "The man who was here this morning is still in my head." He has discovered that now an inner image can form without any outer cause. New capabilities that wish to be activated are at his disposal. They are the same forces that previously structured his body and internal organs, predisposing their forms and functions. After the change of teeth, the only organic activities these forces are responsible for are further physical growth and maintaining life processes. Therefore, a portion of these growth forces (Rudolf Steiner described them as *Bildekräfte* are freed for other tasks. Now, however, they structure and form in the mental domain.

The imagination wants to be addressed with images.

In school one meets the needs of imagination by teaching, wherever appropriate, using clear, descriptive images in order to address the forces of imagination and fantasy. It may begin with little things. For instance, a first grade teacher might ask the class to put a padlock on their mouths instead of being content with "Be quiet!" But, above all, the teacher will familiarize the children with the most important pictorial world there is: fairy tales. Every folk group on Earth has its own rich treasure of fairy tales. The "building blocks" of these stories come from the real, everyday world known to the children, but they do not follow the same rules. They point to an imaginative world behind it all. All the dangers, tests, and triumphs are representative pictures of the tests and dangers that a soul must pass on its way to a more spiritual world. In this world justice prevails, and the good is victorious.

If a teacher is interrupted with: "There are no such things as giants and gnomes," it is usually enough to point out the incontrovertible fact that there are such things in this story. Sometimes one must emphasize that they cannot be seen with our normal, everyday eyes. Generally, curiosity to know what comes next will win out. If the children are able to slip back into listening (and this lengthier listening time is also an ability that must be slowly cultivated), then the question of believability is soon forgotten.

The so-called "nature stories" have a different function. As a kind of precursor to geography, they tell of rocks, plants, and animals, not in a clinical way, but rather more like fables in which something of their being is expressed. For example, if a daffodil has a conversation with a violet, one can imagine that the daffodil in its yellow splendor feels very much superior until the little violet shyly points out that the daffodil is completely dependent upon its pantry, the bulb, whereas the violet bravely stretches out its tender, little roots into the ground! In that way the violet knows all about what goes on in the earth; that is something the daffodil cannot possibly know. One can be sure that from then on the daffodil and violet will be looked at with totally new interest.

Reprimands, corrections, and all moral education are most effective when presented packaged in a story. Perhaps a child has done something wrong; now the event passes through his mind one more time, as if someone else were the wrongdoer. He can now look at everything from a distance, objectively, and the corrective experience will regulate itself. Of course, storytelling is only one part of the wealth of moral teaching that can take place.

The will is educated by doing.

One always tries to lead the children into a new area of learning by first engaging their will through their own activity, making sure their feeling nature is included, and, finally, allowing their understanding to awaken to what is being presented. In this way a child will gradually take part in the things they can do and what they know, as a whole person.

A few, small examples: When teaching writing, again, it is pictures that are put to use; but this time they are pictures that incorporate the forms of the letters of the alphabet drawn on the blackboard by the teacher. The first graders copy the drawings, discover the letter forms, and then "take the forms into their bodies" by first walking the forms on the floor, then drawing them in the air or with their hands on paper, before they ever take up a thick pencil. Such consciously led movements, guided from the inside out, now belong to the newly gained abilities that were previously practiced through form drawing.

But some students have long known the alphabet letters. A teacher is consoled: "But now I can do them right." They no longer appear as random symbols, but rather have an understandable origin.

With arithmetic, it is the feet, and also clapping hands, that first come to know the ever lengthening times tables. If it is structured rhythmically by emphasizing every second or third step, for instance, one gets the times tables that are later committed to memory. The operations of arithmetic are introduced so that, for instance, in addition, one starts with the whole sum, which is divided, thereby allowing something to be given away. A different mental gesture is associated with this than when part after part is piled up.

Cultivating memory requires special care. That means it must be challenged and trained. After all, it is memory that safeguards our personality, the I-consciousness. In a time when everything is stored and retrievable, the memory is almost always neglected.

The world speaks through the teacher.

Whatever is learned or told, it is the teacher through whom the world speaks. The teacher will very naturally become the responsible authority in all matters. This does not mean an ordered or forced authority, but rather one that is loved and also needed. At this age, out of healthy egoism, children are searching for people they can respect and admire, whose judgments they can appropriate for themselves, whose feelings they can "borrow." They need this orientation not only to become knowledgeable, but also for their moral and aesthetic sense. Children are overburdened if they are expected to make decisions prematurely.

A small scene: A mother wants to be especially solicitous and asks her daughter every morning: "What do you want to wear today?" One day her daughter stamps her foot and yells: "I don't want to always have to say what I want to wear!" During another incident, after the mother has reprimanded her child for something, she hears, to her surprise: "Why didn't you tell me I couldn't?" While in the first seven years, the children want a good role model that they can imitate, now they desire an authority figure whom they can follow.

Of course, guidelines that go by age apply only in a very general sense, and are always adjusted according to individual needs. However, today one notices a decided tendency toward "always earlier." One of the reasons for this is the social conditions and civil environment that require awareness and independence from children already at a very early age. Another reason is the opinion that early schooling benefits educational progress throughout the school years. The opposite is true. Early learning happens at the expense of forces that still should be in use for building up the physical body. Granted, the damages are not immediately apparent. And the cognitive abilities are brought into an illusory bloom that disappears in the upper grades and cannot connect itself with the whole person. – from *Erziehungskunst,* April 2010

REFERENCES:
Rudolf Steiner: *The Education of the Child in the Light of Anthroposophy,* GA 34, Dornach 1987.
_____. *Education of the Child,* GA 294, Dornach 1990.
_____. *Education of the Child,* from the Lectures, GA 295, Dornach 1984.

About the Author: Rosemarie Wermbter was born in 1921. A certified librarian, she attended the teachers training course for Waldorf schools, and from 1950 was a class teacher at the Uhlandshöhe Waldorf School in Stuttgart, Germany. Later, she supervised the library for the teachers training seminar and helped publish the Lehrerrundbrief, a monthly publication for Waldorf teachers.

The Fairy Tale of the Crystal Ball

A Path Toward a New Thinking

by Christianne Brown*
translated by Brigitte Knaack

A fairy tale's authenticity can be measured by its potential to charm and captivate, but also by its potential to evoke rejection. An intuitive awareness of quality and a sensibility to the precious gem buried underneath the fairy tale's simple appearance make us receptive to its message, whereas the intellect's inability to think in images may be responsible for a lack of appreciation and understanding. Some modern editions of fairy tales with their corruptions of traditional texts give evidence to such lack of understanding. An unacknowledged fear of the inner realm of the spirit appears to be the main reason for our helplessness in relation to images.

> Poems are like painted windowpanes!
> In gloomy dark the church remains,
> If from the market place you view them:
> That's how the dilettante peers through them.
> Therefore, his mind is glum and shrouded,
> And all his life his eyes are clouded.
> But if you care to come inside
> To greet the holy chapel here,
> You'll find its colors bright and clear.
> Each ornament, each chandelier
> Is flooded now with precious light.
> God's children, come and claim the prize.[1]

---

*Several attempts to contact Christianne Brown have failed. I would appreciate an up-to-date e-mail address from anyone who knows her. – Ed.

Johann Wolfgang von Goethe's metaphorical characterization of the poem may also be applied to fairy tale images: They are like "painted window-panes," whose beauty does not shine forth unless they are illumined by the light of the interior. If modern human beings were to enter this inner realm, they could discover entirely new spiritual perspectives for themselves and for the world.

Where does the fairy tale lead us?

Its path leads us out of the "parentally" guarded world through temptation and error toward truth, through fear and peril of death into a new realm of life. In superior style the fairy tale takes the hurdles placed by the limits of modern consciousness of space and time. In this respect the effort to gain a deeper understanding of fairy tales can become an exercise toward a spirit-filled expansion of our physical-material consciousness.

To reflect on fairy tales is to reflect on images—on images that have been experienced, not just invented. These images have their origin in the ancient mysteries of ancient peoples, taught and experienced in the so-called "academies" of antiquity. The purpose of these mystery schools, whose wisdom echoes in myths and fairy tales, was human self-education. Like any good teacher, the fairy tale accompanies the human soul from the unconsciousness of its instinctive state toward the consciousness of its thinking state, guiding and strengthening it thereby for a future worthy of human beings.

> Whether as the result of diligent scientific study, or whether instinctively, when imparting their wisdom, the Egyptian sages do not use written alphabetic characters, which are imitations of voice and speech, for expressing their teachings and principles. Instead, they draw pictures, and in their temples they record the thought content that goes with each separate thing in hieroglyphic pictures, so that each picture is the embodiment of a specific content of knowledge and wisdom, an object and an integrity that transcend explanation and discussion. The content is then elicited from the picture and expressed in words, and the reason is found why it is as it is, and not otherwise.[2]

The fairy tale of the crystal ball does not merely tell of enchantment—it enchants! The listening soul, spellbound by the fascinating chain of events, is drawn into the magic ring that encircles beginning and end of the tale—opening with the figure of the enchantress, mother of three sons, and closing with the figure of the enchanter, father of the princess. All the figures that move within the field of tension between enchanter and enchantress—with one exception—are prevented from showing their true forms.

However, within this oppressive circle the forces start to move. And the more the outer magical force makes itself felt, the stronger, the more dramatic, the more ready for battle becomes the inner urge for liberation. In fact, the more dramatic the battle becomes, the smaller and more endangered becomes the contested substance: *the crystal ball*. Only one of the figures, *the youngest*, follows his path with unwavering courage. With intuitive wakefulness he escapes from the magic power of the mother to start off on his path toward reuniting what had been separated.

Exactly who are all those appearing and disappearing figures of this heart-stirring soul drama? Which force is symbolized by the *witch*? Who are *the three* who belong together as intimately as sincerely loving brothers? Who is *the third*? What is concealed in the image of *the two giants quarreling about an old hat*? What is portrayed in the mysterious *mirror encounter on the high mountain*? What is pictured in the *elemental struggles* which result in ever new conditions and configurations, and eventually, what is the significance of the threefold image of transformation?

1. The *death of the bull* becomes the element of transformation into the *firebird*.
2. The *fear of the bird* becomes the impulse toward the *birth of the egg*.
3. The *shock brought about by the water* becomes the stimulant for the process of *crystallization*.

Let us now focus our attention on the image of the witch. Another fairy tale image that appears to people of our modern age as far from reality as that of the witch is hard to find and yet on closer inspection we will realize that the witch is one of the key motifs and can help us to decipher the deeper meaning of the fairy tale riddle.

The German word for witch is *Hexe*; it is derived from the Old High German word *hagazussa*.[3] In mythological times she was the wise old woman, the old *hag*, the prophetess, the priestess and clairvoyant guardian of her tribe. By virtue of her motherly authority, she guarded the borders of her family. (Old High German *hag*: an area secured by a *hedge*; German *hecke*: hedge).

While humanity was passing through its childhood phase, absolute power was vested in spiritual authorities (gods, guru-priests, kings, etc.) over their authority-seeking, spiritually dependent pupils. This was quite legitimate during that particular period of human development. As the child approaches the end of his childhood, he wants to leave his "mythological" enclosure and free himself from parental authority to become his own authority. In like manner humanity at large arrived at the end of its childhood period and entered a new phase of development during which the clairvoyant matriarchal claim of the mother (the hagazussa) to guard and to guide lost its legitimacy. Humanity wanted to wake up to its own independence. Wherever the hagazussa was not willing to give up her claim to authority, her originally benevolent white magic changed into destructive black magic. The hagazussa became the *witch*.

If we now proceed to "elicit the content from the picture," as the Greek philosopher Plotinus describes it, we realize: *The witch is the force within myself that resists development and anxiously clings to the old.*

There is a spiritual principle though: the law of change and renewal. What is right for a particular time and for a particular state of consciousness may be wrong at a later stage of development; it may even turn into the opposite. Carried over into our modern human situation this means: Old paths of teaching and old methods of training (yoga, TM, drugs, etc.), which may have been necessary at some time in the past for the development of the childlike-mythological human consciousness, are no longer appropriate for our modern consciousness. They may even be harmful.

> The witch's eyes were red [and dim], and she could not see very far, but she had a keen scent, like the beasts. ...[4]

Translated into our language this means: the old magic consciousness is an instinctive consciousness. The spiritual is "sensed," not apprehended as the result of clear-sighted and open-minded thinking. The red, short-sighted eyes of the witch are the dim counterpart of the crystal-clear ball, whose sparkling light finds its reflection in the mirror of truth on the mountain, in the tears of the grief-stricken princess, and in the well at the foot of the mountain, which is guarded and barred by the bull.[5]

Now the first sentences of the fairy tale gain meaning:

> There was once an enchantress who had three sons who loved each other as brothers, but the old woman did not trust them, and thought they wanted to steal her power from her. So she changed the eldest into an eagle, which was forced to dwell in the rocky mountains … The second, she changed into a whale, which lived in the deep sea. …The third son, who was afraid she might change him into a raging wild beast, a bear perhaps, or a wolf, went secretly away.

When the fairy tale speaks of "three brothers" or "three sons," it alludes to three fundamental human soul forces that sometimes work together and at other times work against each other. It has taken a long time to develop the free I-personality in individual human beings as well as in humanity at large. The sensitive, feeling human being is the eldest son and brother—the I in feeling. Then the faculty of thinking evolved. The intelligently thinking human being is the second son and brother—the I in thinking. The consciously willing human being is the third and youngest son and brother—the I in willing.

With great caution we may suspect that during the course of oral tradition an error has crept in with regard to the sequence of the animal transformations.[6] To restore this transformational scene to its proper significance the respective lines should read as follows:

> … so she changed the eldest into a whale, which lived in the deep sea ….

Even though the fish in the water is regarded as an image for spiritual experience, it stands for experiences of a more emotional nature, "emerging out of the depths" of the soul, rather than for experiences of the high-altitude flight of keen perception. The water in this context is the element of the "surging rush of emotion" and of the dark unconscious.

> The second, she changed into an eagle, which was forced to dwell in the rocky mountains [of the skull], and was often seen sweeping in great circles in the sky.

The image of the eagle usually signifies spirit in motion, spirit wind that elevates human thinking and supports it on its high-altitude flight providing thus the "overview" of "keen perception." Consider this image in comparison with the Horus falcon at the back of the Egyptian pharaoh's head, or think of the American Indian's crown of feathers.

> The third son, who was afraid she might change him into a raging wild beast [of the earth]... went secretly away.

After all, the power of will can be called human only if it has overcome the animal instincts, for example the fear instinct, the survival instinct, the herd instinct, etc.

The instinctive wild drives, symbolized in fairy tales by "wild animals," are active in human beings, too, even in small children. However, if an individual strives to lead a life worthy of a human being, he must learn to be master of his instincts and transform them into I-conscious will. This is exactly what the fairy tale describes when the youngest brother escapes the danger of being dominated by his instincts, thanks to his intuitive wakefulness. Instead, he finds himself confronted with the wild animal at a later time. He struggles with it and finally kills it with the sword that was not his own at the beginning of his path. It is noteworthy in this connection that the bull fights practiced in earlier cultures, e.g., those of the Persian Mithras Mysteries, were exercises to gain mastery and control over these instincts. I will come back to this subject in a later paragraph.

Well aware that development may lead to liberation, the witch is afraid of losing her position of power. Therefore, she tries to prevent the unfolding individuation of the I in feeling, thinking and willing, namely the three fundamental forces of the soul, which are united "in brotherly love." She isolates thinking from feeling and banishes each of them into its extreme. If thinking is not complemented by the warming touch of feeling, the soul must suffer harm. The other extreme, pure emotion without the ordering activity of thinking, is just as tragic. Modern psychology describes this phenomenon as *split personality*. The witch misjudged the outcome of her manipulation. Her attempt to prevent the brothers' development has quite the opposite effect: it initiates a process of true discrimination and self-realization. Like Mephistopheles in Goethe's *Faust,* she is "a part of that force which would do evil evermore, and yet creates the good."

The youngest soul force, the will, goes on his way with great determination:

> By chance he came into a great forest, and did not know the way out of it. All at once he saw in the distance two giants …

When the fairy tale has its hero wander through landscapes, enter a forest, climb a mountain, it never speaks of geographical locations but about transitional stages of changing soul realms. The forest is a world of proliferous vitality. Passions can easily erupt there in the shape of wild beasts or giants. It is usually dark in there and hardly ever does one know how one got in and even less how to get out. With other words, it is a world of harrying overabundance of wild forces of growth and, at the same time, a world of dark and dim semi-consciousness, even unconsciousness.

The giant is the embodiment of prehistoric, mythological man, Adam Kadmon, whose superhuman enormous figure and physical strength reach "from the earth up unto the stars."[7] He has a small head though, which means he lacks the faculties of alert, intellectual thinking and discernment.

> The small men are cleverer than we are, so we will leave the decision to thee.

The hat covers the head. It represents the activity of thinking, brain-thinking, and in most fairy tales it is a key element for the course of action. *Red Riding Hood* is so fond of her little hood that she never takes it off. *Cinderella* asks her father, the merchant, to bring her as a gift the first hazel twig that strikes against his hat. *The Star Money* is the story of a homeless child who gives her hood to the child who is asking for it because his "head is so cold."

As the hat keeps out the influx from above, so does one-sided head-thinking. By focusing on concepts and definitions, it establishes clear and one-sided barriers to the spiritual. A subconscious perception of this is mirrored in secular customs as well as in religious-cultic traditions. Consider, for instance, the respectful gesture of taking one's hat off in the presence of a king or God, in church, in meeting and greeting another person, or the gesture of covering the head as an expression of self-responsibility: "On my head be it."

In our story the giants quarrel about an old hat. The qualities of this hat are not known to the youngest son and when he makes use of its power he does so unconsciously. The old hat, the wishing-hat, represents the "old" thinking, the magical wish-thinking, which was able to overcome space and time but did not yet make use of the brain. It is a requisite of the old magic-maternal world of the giants, which as it is falling apart creates disunity and disharmony because the principle of the three, the principle of development, is alien to it. The quarrel of the two giants and the separation of the brothers are symbolic of this process.[8] In naïve innocence the youngest brother continues on his way, following his *own* resolve to deliver the princess, forgetful of the world of the giants as he leaves them behind. Note that he is not flying but making use of his own feet.

> He thought of the King's daughter, forgot the giants, and walked continually onward.

Although in our text the feet are not specifically mentioned, it is still worthwhile to direct our attention to the symbols of "foot" and "shoe" because implicitly the story talks about them: " ... went secretly away" ... "and walked continually onward." On his feet and in his shoes the human being stands upon the earth. They are symbols of our connection with the earthly and hence with the tasks and possibilities of life. The one who is wearing only one shoe does no longer fully stand in life; the one who is wearing *shoes full of holes* has lost important faculties and is incompetent in life. *Worn-out shoes* indicate that a path has come to an end. *Chopped-off toes* signify an extremely materialistic path of life; *chopped-off heels* signify an escapist, dreamy attitude.[9]

If we want to discover our own humanity we need to rise, and wherever we rise we must also face the possibility of falling. The bigger and more impatient the expectation, the greater the illusion and disappointment. What bitter disappointment awaits our hero on entering the *Castle of the Golden Sun* up on the mountain! Highest expectations! Almost at the destination—and still so far from it!

Few fairy tales can rival the *Crystal Ball* in intensity, sophistication and intelligence. An almost overwhelming abundance of soul experiences, questions and insights are concentrated in this short encounter with the spellbound princess, who is waiting for her redemption, and in the intimate conversation with her.

Above: in the empty castle, dwindled forces of life and stifled development.
However: in the midst of this grey and empty magic world, a spark of light: the crystal-clear, undisturbed mirror of truth and cognition.

> …this is not my form; human eyes can only see me in this state of ugliness, but that thou mayst know what I am like, look in the mirror. It does not let itself be misled—it will show thee my image as it is in truth.

Below: by the spring: surging, always self-renewing forces of life.
However: kept in the dark, made inaccessible and guarded by the wild bull, the animal.

Above: bitter disappointment after a strenuous journey.
However: in spite of doubt and fear, determination and will for action, readiness for the spiritual leap from bitterness to the question:

> How canst thou be set free? I fear no danger. …Nothing can keep me from doing it, but tell me what I must do.[10]

Below: grave danger to life.
However: the first independent deed after being given a visionary answer.

With the death of the bull the soul drama is set in motion. Not only is the stream of vital energy set free and starts to surge anew, but the whole scenery becomes a spectacle of tremendous elemental turmoil.

As every birth is preceded by an experience of death, so also does the death of the bull act as a catalyst for a threefold birth of ever-new states of fire. Out of the fiery power of the bull the fiery bird is born. The light of the fiery bird in turn intensifies and transforms into the burning egg. Yet, only under tremendous pressure exerted by brother Eagle is the egg released from the bird's body. The fire catastrophe expected to follow upon the threefold fiery metamorphosis is prevented by the cooling waves of the sea churned up by brother Whale. At last, the undamaged crystal ball can be taken out of the broken shell.

Special attention is due to the image of the bull who guards the well. Out of his body the fiery bird is born and next to him stands the youngest brother with the sword in his hand. This image is a true reflection of one of the central initiation experiences of the ancient mysteries. The bull is the symbol of the forces of life and growth, the forces of renewal and fertility.

In ancient Egypt the sacred bull Apis was regarded as the tangible symbol of these forces. Later, during the Greek epoch, in Crete, the festival of "Jumping over the Bull" was celebrated. "Skilled young men confronted the bull, grabbed its horns and vaulted over its back."[11]

A later form of conquering the bull was practiced in the Persian Mithras Mysteries, whose central experience was the victory of the light over the darkness. Mithras, the son of the sun, conquers the bull by the well by sitting on his back and thrusting his sword into the back of its neck. Also, this is how the cultic cave paintings depict it. This image is not intended to glorify destruction as a form of self-gratification; instead, it points to the transformation of the dull forces of nature into the light of consciousness, which in our fairy tale is represented by the fiery bird. In the ancient mystery schools the phoenix was a symbol of instruction, the bird of thought, which, according to tradition, consumes itself by fire every five hundred years and rises anew from the ashes.

We encounter the phoenix again in Phoenicia, a country named after it. There it is described as having wings of gold or wings that shine in all the colors of the rainbow, and its nest is believed to spread a pleasant aroma of cinnamon. This cult was known throughout the world of antiquity. The conquering of the bull and the resurrection of the phoenix were parts of the central initiation experiences of antiquity. They represent what many centuries later reappears in the following words by Goethe as the ripe fruit of his genius:

> And as long as you do not quest
> For this "Die and bring to birth!"
> You are but a somber guest
> On the darkling earth.

The death of the bull and the rise of the phoenix are images that cast special light on one of the most interesting phenomena of the ancient world: the schools of initiation and their methods. The tremendous achievements of the spiritual elite of that time inspire us with great respect, and so we will describe with the greatest caution some aspects of the initiation proceedings as they are reflected in the fairy tale of the crystal ball. The mystery schools were the spiritual centers of antiquity and they were common throughout the world: *Heliopolis* and *Memphis* in Egypt; *Eleusis, Delphi, Ephesus* and *Samothrace* in Greece; the *Externsteine* in the Teutoburg forest in Germany; then *Chartres* in France, to name just a few of them.

Long before Christianity made its entry, Chartres was the center of Celtic druidism. Once a year all Druid priests would come together there to gather by the holy wells and in front of the portrait of the *Virgo Paritura*, the virgin about to give birth. Like all initiates they were the teachers of a chosen group of young people. They taught the elite of their time, and from their vast experience and their profound understanding of nature, they gave instructions regarding seeding and harvesting. They also taught subjects such as geology, astronomy, philosophy and religion. After a period of about ten years the students were ready to leave the school and act as intermediaries between the center of teaching and the uninitiated-the common people. These bards, as they were called, travelled all over the western and northwestern Celtic region and presented the content of their mystery experiences in so-called didactic songs.

In this ancient bardic tradition, we find not only the origin of all European myths and fairy tales, but also the origin of the profession of the storyteller. The bard presented his fairy tales with modesty. Out of reverence for the content of the tales nothing was omitted or added to embellish the stories. Changes of text, omissions, abridged versions and modernizations began only within the last three hundred years, when the healthy intuition in regard to the quality of the original texts of the fairy tales became weaker and weaker and eventually threatened to become extinct.

We can say with certainty that old fairy tale images are not merely accidental images but symbols. They certainly did not come about as a result of random associations ... of a foggy folk-fantasy. Instead, these symbols are well-balanced and precise. ... An indication of this is the strictly objectified art form of the fairy tale as well as the fact that quite often images of mythological processes have been transformed and transposed into the form of the fairy tale.[12]

One can assume that the guiding impulses and principles for human life at that time, in particular all rules of physical and spiritual conduct, came from the mystery centers and the people who were trained by them. There we find the origin of our natural sciences, agriculture and medicine, of architecture, social sciences and religion. Influential personalities like *Heraclitus, Empedocles, Plato, Aristotle, Plutarch* and *Plotin*—they all were students of the mysteries. The mystery centers were the carriers and initiators of human culture for many thousands of years; nevertheless, for the world outside everything that went on in these schools was shrouded in mystery. The little knowledge we have about these schools has come down to us by way of cryptographic fragments of the wisdom that was strictly supervised and guarded by the mystery priests.

All those who were not satisfied with folk religion and its traditions searched for and found the teachers in the mysteries. These individuals would then withdraw completely from everyday life and submit their souls to a preparatory discipline of renunciation, including rituals of washing, wearing special garments and abstaining from certain types of meat. Under the guidance of twelve priestly assistants, the hierophant was guided from stage to stage and accompanied on his way toward ever deeper knowledge of himself. During a period of three and a half days, he was lifted out of his physical body to such a degree that, although his bodily functions could still be maintained, in a deathlike sleep his soul went through trauma, fear and illusion. Through purposefully guided experiences of shock, for which the neophyte prepared for many years, the soul was led to the limits of its own capacity and beyond into the deeply individual experience of the immortal I. Since these extremely difficult inner experiences were contingent on the personal response of the particular individual to the purposefully guided traumatic experiences, the hierophant had to make a solemn promise of secrecy to guard against corruption by the uninitiated. Betrayal of the mysteries was forbidden on penalty of death.

Aeschylus, the famous Greek dramatist, is known to have been accused of betraying initiation secrets in his plays, but when he was summoned before court, he was able to prove that he had never been a student of the mysteries.

It was permitted to describe the student's central experience (here that of the Eleusinian Mysteries) in the following words:

I have come to the bounds of death and set foot on the threshold of Proserpine; I passed through all the elements and returned; at midnight I saw the sun shining in dazzling-white light; I saw the gods above and below from face to face and worshipped them at close range.[14]

Many other images that occur again and again in myths and fairy tales indicate that they depict initiation experiences: images of wandering, passing through fire, passing through ice, swimming in or through water (ocean or river), terrifying images of the drawn sword and of flowing blood. We also learn about the "homelessness" of the "son," about the "father" who abandons the son in a "boat." King and queen, bridegroom and bride, widow and children of the widow, hazelnut and oak tree, fish and bee—they are all symbols of different stages of the path of initiation. We learn about the desperate search of Gilgamesh, King of Uruk, for the "light of the sun" in the "dark mountain," of "twelve leagues," of threatening "animals," and ultimately we learn of death and overcoming it, after which the hierophant is allowed to come near to the god![15]

During initiation the physical human being goes through death and gives birth to the spiritual, the divine being within. Among the numerous examples of initiation fairy tales, I would like to mention two that have special significance for further study: Grimm's *The King of the Golden Mountain* and *The King's Son Who Feared Nothing*.

Another wonderful description of an initiation experience can be found in the account given by the prophet Jonah of his experience "in the belly of the great fish."

For thou hadst cast me into the deep, in the midst of the seas; and the floods compassed me about: all thy billows and thy waves passed over me. Then I said, I am been cast out of thy sight; yet I will look again toward thy holy temple [my own innermost being]. The waters compassed me about, even to the soul: the depth closed me round about, the weeds were wrapped about my head. I went down to the bottoms of the mountains; the earth with her bars was about me for ever: yet hast thou brought up my life from corruption, O Lord my God [who art thyself my innermost, concealed being]. When my soul fainted [when I set my soul free] within me, I remembered the Lord [the Lord of all worlds shone forth within me]: and my prayer came in unto thee, into thine holy temple.[16]

And more than two thousand years after Jonah, the Persian-Arabic image of the phoenix bird was still alive and permeated the alchemy of that period:

> Be pure of soul and dust become
> That from your dust may shoot up grass.
> Are you then hay, consume yourself
> That from your embers light may glow.
> And are you then mere burnt-up dust
> Your ashes are the wise man's stone.[17]

The well-guarded secret of the alchemist method of producing a substance called the "philosopher's stone" through a process of transmutation brings us back to our fairy tale of the crystal ball. As we look closely at the "birth processes" in the fairy tale we come to realize that they are accounts of true alchemist processes.

> The emergence of the crystal ball bears a striking resemblance—even to the most fascinating details—to the natural formation of a diamond under the influence of atmospheric pressure, fire and water. A mineralogist will tell us that a natural diamond burns when exposed to high atmospheric pressure and temperatures of more than 8000° Celsius, provided that at the time of this extremely heated state it is also exposed to a strong current of oxygen, i.e., when it comes in contact with air that has a high concentration of oxygen.[18]

If we do not content ourselves with merely enjoying the poetic beauty and the symbolic diversity of this fairy tale but are prepared to receive some wondrous new tidings (the essence of what is "told" in the "tale"), then we must deepen our understanding of the image of the crystal ball. As it happens so often when we try to understand a fairy tale image, language can put us on the right track. It speaks of "sharp" and "crystal-clear" thinking, a thinking that can injure with its sharpness but can also help to clarify something. The thinking implied here is the logical-intellectual thinking, which has a deadening effect when used exclusive of other soul forces, even in areas that cannot be illumined, analyzed and grasped by the intellect. This is implied in our fairy tale when it warns against the mineral's potential forces of destruction.

> ... and if it fall on the ground [without the cooling effect of the water element], it will flame up and burn everything that is near.[19] He who gets the crystal ball and holds it before the enchanter will destroy his power with it.

We have already come to know the magician's power over the forces of life and growth, but what is the nature of the power of the crystal ball? What is its hidden secret? The secret of the crystal ball lies in the amalgamation of two extremes: the radial-crystalline and the spherical-globular. We will not find a single spherical crystal formation in inanimate nature; such a form is created by human hands only. Wherever a natural crystal does have a tendency toward the spherical, it always occurs at the price of losing its transparency, of losing the light. Wherever nature exhibits spherical formations, they come about through contact with the rounding action of water—and water is life!

Two forces are confronting each other: the life force of the crystal ball and the magic power over life—the force of living, "pure" thinking and the magic power of instinctive-magical consciousness.

The fairy tale of the crystal ball is an appeal to us to strive for a new thinking that has the potential to heal the distress experienced by human souls in our time. If this new thinking is contended for with fearless will—as shown in the fairy tale—it is able to join together what had been separated, to humanize what had been bestial, to give light to that which had been dark, breaking thus the magic resistance against renewal and growth.

Our ordinary thinking is passive thinking. Usually stimulated by sense perceptions, it is a projection of the outer world.[20] Most of the experiences carried about in our souls have been stimulated from outside. As a rule, our thinking is not active but re-active, initiated by desires, fears, calculations of profit and loss, but most of all determined by habit. By contrast, active thinking is original thinking, independent thinking, a spiritual act of creation accomplished by the strength and effort of our free human will, independent of the outer world of the senses.

Our fairy tale teaches us the first steps on the path toward stimulating this new creative thinking and thereby toward redeeming our human "royal" dignity.

1. Free yourself from any inappropriate claim of authority!
2. Be not afraid!
3. Do not attach more value to the "old hat" than is due to it today!
4. Do not see through "human eyes" only, but look into the mirror of truth!
5. Be not afraid to ask questions!
6. Be not afraid of unaccustomed answers!
7. Conquer the beast!

I am well aware that this attempt at interpreting the fairy tale *The Crystal Ball* is giving just one aspect of many. Additional aspects of the initiation rites, e.g., the so-called trials of fire, water and air, would show us quite different paths again; however, this would go beyond the scope of this article. Therefore, I have confined myself to the leading theme, the evolution of human thinking, which, although endangered by the one-sided training of the intellect, can be healed by imaginative pictorial thinking. In that sense the fairy tale of the crystal ball—in fact every fairy tale—is message and exercise at the same time.

ENDNOTES:
1. Johann Wolfgang von Goethe (1749-1832), German poet.
2. Plotinus (205-270 AD), Greek philosopher, who founded Neoplatonism.
3. Friedl Lenz, *Bildsprache der Märchen*.
4. Grimm's *Complete Fairy Tales*, "Hansel and Gretel."
5. The Hebrew word *ajin* means *eye*, but it also stands for *mirror* and *well*.
6. Friedl Lenz, *Bildsprache der Märchen*.
7. *The Legends of the Jews*.
8. The relationship between *magic* and *mother* has its etymological origin in the Sanskrit root *mah: mater; mater magna* as the expression for the earth, Mother Earth. *Magic*: control over the force of life. Maya: the goddess of the force of life (also called Majesta) and the goddess of the month of May, the month of the burgeoning vitality of Spring.
9. Compare the two stepdaughters in the fairy tale "Cinderella."
10. Medieval Parzival fails to ask the ailing King Anfortas the redeeming question and is therefore considerably set back on his path of development, while the King is condemned to further suffering.
11. Ortrud Stumpfe, *Die Symbolsprache der Märchen*.
12. Ibid.
13. Rudolf Steiner, *Christianity as Mystical Fact* (GA 8).
14. Lucius Apuleius (c. 125–200 AD), Roman philosopher and writer.

15. It is interesting to note that the Gilgamesh epic tells about an unsuccessful initiation.
16. *Bible* (King James Version), Jonah 2: 3–7.
17. Feerid-eddin-Attar (1216–1313) Persian Sufi.
18. Rudolf Geiger, *Märchenkunde*.
19. The fairy tale has created a number of other images to express the nature of the intellect.
20. • The activity of the tailor with needle and scissors is a fitting image for an intellectual attitude. He strikes at wholeness, cuts it into pieces and puts them together again at his own discretion. His *modus operandi* is analysis and synthesis.
    • The woodcutter personifies the abstract theoretician, who analyses and splits concepts, losing sight of the living whole.
    • The coldness of the intellect is well-expressed in the image of "the grave of the rich man's wife, which is covered with snow."

Grimm Fairy Tale #197
The Crystal Ball

Once upon a time there was a sorceress who had three sons, and they loved each other dearly. But the old woman did not trust them and thought they wanted to steal her power. So she changed the oldest son into a eagle. He had to make his home in the mountain cliffs, and sometimes he could be seen gliding up and down in the sky and making circles. The second son was changed into a whale that lived deep in the ocean, and one could see him only when he sometimes sent mighty jets of water high into the air. Both sons reverted to their human shape for just two hours every day. Since the third son feared that his mother might change him also, this time into a wild animal, perhaps a bear or a wolf, he sneaked away in secret.

Indeed, he had heard that at the castle of the golden sun there was an enchanted princess who was waiting to be rescued. However, one would have to risk one's life. Twenty-tree young men had already suffered a miserable death, and only one more would be allowed to try to rescue her. After that nobody would be permitted to come. Since he had a courageous heart, he decided to search for the castle of the golden sun.

He had already traveled a long time and had not been able to find it, when he got lost in a large forest and could not find his way out. Suddenly he noticed two giants in the distance, who waved to him with their hands, and as he approached them they said, "We're quarreling over this hat and who should get it. Since we're each just as strong as the other, neither one can defeat the other. Now, small people are smarter than we are, so we want you to make the decision."

"How can you quarrel over an old hat?" the young man asked.

"You don't know the powers it has. It's a wishing hat. Whoever puts it on can wish himself to be anywhere he wants, and within seconds he'll be there."

"Give me the hat," the young man said. "I'll go off some distance from here, and when I call you, run to me, and whoever wins the race will get the hat." He put the hat on his head and went off. However, he thought about the king's daughter, forgot the giants, and kept going. Once he sighed with all his heart and cried out, "Oh, if only I were at the castle of the golden sun!" And no sooner had he uttered these words than he was standing on top of a high mountain in front of the castle gate.

He entered the castle and strode through all the rooms until he reached the last one, where he found the king's daughter. However, he was horrified when he saw her: Her face was ash gray and full of wrinkles, and she had dreary eyes and red hair. "Are you the king's daughter whose beauty is praised by the entire world?" he exclaimed.

"Ah," she replied, "this is not my real condition. Human eyes can see me only in this ugly form. But look into this mirror so you'll know what I look like. The mirror can't be fooled, and it will show you my image as it truly is."

She handed him the mirror, and he saw the reflection of the most beautiful maiden in the world, and he saw tears rolling down her cheeks out of sadness. Then he said, "How can you be saved? I'm afraid of nothing."

She replied, "Whoever gets the crystal ball and holds it in front of the magician will break his power, and I'll return to my true form. But," she added, "many a man has gone to his death because of this, and you, my young thing, I'd feel sorry if you placed yourself in such great danger."

"Nothing can stop me," he said. "But tell me what I must do."

"I want you to know everything," the king's daughter answered. "When you descend the mountain on which the castle stands, there'll be a wild bison at the bottom next to the spring. You will have to fight it. And, if you should be so fortunate as to slay this beast, a firebird will rise from it. This bird carries a glimmering egg in its body, and the egg has a crystal ball as a yolk. However, the bird will not let go of the egg unless it is forced to. And, if the egg falls onto the ground, it will set everything on fire and destroy everything near it. The egg itself will melt along with the crystal ball, and all your efforts will have been in vain."

The young man descended the mountain and reached the spring, where the bison snorted and roared at him. After a long battle the young man pierced the bison's body with his sword, and the beast sank to the ground. The firebird immediately rose from the bison and tried to fly away, but the eagle, the brother of the young man, who flew through the clouds, dived after the bird and chased it toward the ocean.

There the eagle hit the bird so hard with its beak that the bird was forced to let the egg fall. However, it did not fall into the ocean but on top of a fisherman's hut standing on the shore, and the hut began to smoke right away and was about to burst into flames. Then waves as large as houses rose up in the ocean, swept over the hut, and vanquished the flames. The second brother, the whale, had swum toward the shore and driven the water onto the land.

When the fire was out, the young man searched for the egg and was fortunate enough to find it. It had not melted yet, but the shell had cracked open due to the sudden cooling from the water, and he could take out the crystal ball, which was undamaged.

When the young man went to the magician and held the ball in front of him, the magician said, "My power is destroyed. From now on you are king of the castle of the golden sun. You can also restore your brothers to their human form."

So the young man hurried back to the king's daughter, and as he entered her room she stood there in all her magnificent beauty, and they exchanged rings with each other in a joyful celebration.

Interpreting Fairy Tales

by Rudolf Steiner
translated by Anna Meuss

Today we will work with the principles with which we can interpret fairy tales, sagas, and in a larger context, mythology. I will explain what should live in the soul of the person who tells the tales—what he should know. First, we must realize that we need to know a lot more than we actually tell the children. Secondly, the ways of explaining the tales must be brought out of our understanding of anthroposophical wisdom. Perhaps the first fairy tale may be told like this:

Something happened once. Yes, where did it happen? Well, we can also ask where did it not happen? Once upon a time there lived a tailor apprentice. He had only one groschen in his wallet but it was enough to drive him to undertake a journey. He became hungry and the groschen could buy him only a bowl of milk soup. As the milk soup was placed before him, a swarm of flies flew into the soup. When he emptied the bowl it was completely covered. With his hand the apprentice hit the flies in the bowl a couple of times and counted how many he smashed. It was one hundred. On the waiter's little slate he wrote: "With one stroke he smashed one hundred!"

He hung the slate around his neck and walked on. Then he passed a King's castle. At that very moment the King looked down from the walls and saw someone walking by with something written on the little blackboard. The King sent his servant down to see what was written there. The servant went below and on the board was written: "With one stroke he smashed one hundred!"

This he told the King. "Stop!" yelled the King, "there is someone I can use." The King sent people down to get the apprentice and bring him into the castle. "I can use you!" proclaimed the King, "Would you like to enter my service?"

"Yes," answered the boy. "I would very much like to enter your service when you give me a good salary that I will tell you later."

"Yes," said the King. "I will pay you well when you deliver on your promises. Therefore you shall eat and drink well, as long as you like. Then you must do me a favor that compares to your strength. In my land every year a whole troupe of bears enters and does tremendous damage. They are so strong that no human being can kill them. You will surely be able to kill them if you keep the promise written on your board."

The apprentice answered, "Of course I will, but before the bears come I will eat and drink as much as I like." He said to himself, *If I cannot smash the bears and they eat me, at least I have eaten and drunk well for awhile.*

As the time came for the bears to reappear, the boy prepared himself. He went into the kitchen and set up a table. On the table were many things bears like to eat and drink, especially honey. He left the door open. He lay down to wait. When the bears walked in they ate and drank until they could not move but lay on the floor. The apprentice hit each one on the head and took care of them.

When the King saw this, he asked, "What did you do?"

And the boy answered, "I let the bears run over the door step and then hit them on the head!"

The King was very gullible and said, "As you have done such a wonderful thing, can you do me an ever greater favor? Every year powerful giants enter our land. No one can kill them or kick them out. Perhaps you are able?"

The tailor apprentice replied, "Yes I will, if you give me your daughter for my bride when I succeed." It was very important for the King to get rid of the giants so he agreed and the boy prepared himself.

When the time came for the giants to appear, the boy took all kinds of things that giants like to eat and drink and walked towards them in the woods. Along the way he also collected a piece of cheese and a skylark. When he arrived where the giants rested, one of them proclaimed, "We are back and ready to fight the strongest people you have. No one has ever beaten us!"

"Very well, then I will fight you," replied the apprentice boy.

One giants commented, "You will be badly beaten."

The boy answered, "Show me your strength. Show me what you can do!"

The giant grabbed a stone and squeezed it between his fingers. He took his bow and an arrow and shot the arrow in the air so it did not come down to earth for a long time. "You wanted to see my strength! If you will challenge me, you'd better bring something new."

The boy picked up a small stone and covered it with the cheese, and as he pressed it with his fingers, the cheese squirted out. He told the giants, "I can press water out of stones and you cannot!" That made a huge impression on the giants. He could do something they could not.

The tailor apprentice took up the bow and arrow, and as he loosed the arrow, he slipped the skylark free without the giants noticing it. The skylark never came back. He told the giants, "Your arrow came back to the earth. Mine was shot so high that it will never return!"

The giants were puzzled: Here was someone stronger than they were, and so they asked him to join them. The boy agreed to be their comrade. He was small but a good addition to their group. They became friends and the boy stayed with them for a while. But it was scary for the giants to have someone stronger in their company and one night, while the boy lay almost asleep on his bed, he heard the giants planning to kill him.

Then he made precautions. He prepared a huge meal with the things he had brought along. The giants ate and drank until they fainted, but they were still ready to kill him. The boy took the intestines of a pig and filled them with blood, tied them around his head, and lay in bed. The giant who was chosen to kill him stuck a hole in the intestine and the blood flowed. This pleased the giants, for now they thought they were rid of the boy, and they lay down to sleep. Immediately the tailor apprentice stood up and killed each one of the sleeping giants.

He went to the King and told him that he had killed the giants one after the other. The King kept his word and gave the boy his daughter for his bride.

The tailor apprentice held a wedding. The King was amazed at the boy's strength, but neither the king nor his daughter knew who the traveling boy truly was. Was he a tailor apprentice or a king's son? Back then they did not know. If they have not learned yet, then they still do not know today.

※

That is the first fairy tale for us to observe. Next to it we want to place another. For when you tell fairy tales, no matter which country or people they come from, there is always a wealth of mental images pulsating through them. We have met the giants who were overcome by cleverness. Take a giant step through the millennia and think into the Odysseus saga about Odysseus and the giant Polyphemus. And we will place another fairy tale next to the first one.

※

Something happened once. Yes, where did it happen? Well, where did it not happen? There was a King who was so loved by his people that he often heard them wish him a wife who was as good and noble as he. It was hard for him to find anyone he could believe in, someone who would be the proper wife for him. But he had a very wise, old friend, a poor forester who lived simply and peacefully in the woods.

The forester could have easily become rich, for the King would have loved to give him everything. But the forester wanted to remain poor and keep his wisdom. The King went to his friend and asked for advice. The forester gave the King a rosemary branch and told him, "Keep this and the girl to whom it bows [consider the divining rod motif] is the girl you shall marry!"

On the next day the King invited many young girls to his court. He placed many pearls on a table and wrote each name of the girls with the pearls. He told them that the one for whom the rosemary bows would be his bride. The others could keep their pearls. He walked around with his rosemary branch but it did not move and it bowed to none of them. The girls received their pearls and were asked to leave.

On the second day the same procedure was repeated but with no success. The same was true on the third day. That night the King slept and heard something at his window. It turned out to be a golden bird that said to him, "You do not know this but you have twice provided me a huge service. I want to do you a favor. When you awake in the morning stand up, take up your rosemary branch and follow me. I will bring you to a place where you will find a horse. The horse will have a silver arrow stuck in its body. You must pull the arrow out of the horse. Then the horse can take you to your new bride!"

The very next morning the King followed the golden bird. The bird led him to the horse that was very weak and sick and complained, "A witch shot the arrow into my body." The King pulled out the arrow and that moment the weak, dying animal was turned into a wonderfully powerful horse. The King mounted the horse with his rosemary branch and commanded the horse forward. With the golden bird flying before them, the King rode the magical horse.

They finally arrived at a glass castle. *Brrm. Brrrrrrm. Brummmmmmm.* Loud noises met them outside. When they entered the castle, the King, the rosemary branch and the golden bird saw the king of the castle covered in glass. In his stomach was a terribly strong bee. This was the source of the noise outside. The bumblebee tried to bore its way out of the Glass King's stomach.

The King asked the Glass King what was happening. "Well," replied the Glass King, "look at the sofa where my Queen sits in a rose-colored silk gown and the secret you will immediately discover. For the spider web from the thorn bush that is woven around the Queen is torn, and soon it will rip apart. When there is no web left, when it is totally gone, the evil spider will spin a new web around my Queen while I remain here spellbound and frozen in glass. We will remain here for hundreds of years until the spell is broken."

This was all true. The evil spider appeared and wrapped up the Queen with his evil web. As the spider was busy spinning its web, the magical horse tried to kill the spider. It tried to step on the spider, and in that moment the bee broke through the glass surrounding the Glass King's stomach and tried to help the spider. But the magic horse killed them both. In that very moment the Glass King was transformed to a human King, the thorn bush was turned into a pretty serving girl, and the Queen was freed from the spider web. The Glass King explained what had happened.

As he was king, he was persecuted by an evil witch who lived in the forest surrounding his kingdom. The witch wanted him to marry her daughter. Yet he had found his wife at the nearby magic castle. The witch swore revenge. She turned the King into glass and his daughter into a bumblebee that bore into his stomach. The Queen was tormented by the witch who turned herself into an evil spider and spun a web around her victim. The servant girl was turned into a thorn bush, and the horse that had picked her up was shot with a silver arrow by the evil witch. But now everything was fine. The magic horse was freed and all of the people.

The King asked the Glass King where he could find a wife who was good for him. He was shown the path to the nearby magical castle. The golden bird flew ahead and when they arrived, it found a lily. The rosemary branch approached the lily and bowed before the beautiful flower. In this moment a beautiful girl arose from the lily that was enchanted, for the Queen of the nearby castle was her sister. Now all of the evil deeds were resolved. The King took her home, where they held a wedding and lived in extraordinary happiness for themselves and their people. They lived a very long time. No one knows for sure. If they have not disappeared or died, then they must still be alive.

⇒⟫⟪⇐

Now we have another fairy tale with another motif. The first mistake we need to overcome when looking into real fairy tales or sagas is the misunderstanding that they are merely fantastical stories from local folklore. That is never the case. The origin of fairy tales lies in very ancient times, in times before mankind developed rational culture but possessed a very high-quality clairvoyance, the remains of a more ancient, original clairvoyance. Those people who retained such clairvoyance experienced states of mind that moved between asleep and awake. When these people were in a state of mind somewhere between sleep and awakened consciousness, they experienced the spiritual world in multiple forms. It was nothing like a dream of today. Dreams today are pretty chaotic for most people but not for everyone. In ancient times, people with clairvoyance experienced something very regular, so regular that the experiences were similar and typical for different folk.

What took place for the people in such transitional states of mind between sleep and being awake? When people are in their physical bodies they experience the world with their physical organs. Behind them is the spiritual world. In the ancient clairvoyant states of mind, it was as if a veil were removed from the people and the lower spiritual world became visible. Whatever took place in the spiritual world stood in relationship to the inner life of human beings. It was just as it was in the physical world: You could not see the colors with your ears or hear the tones with your eyes. What is outside relates to what is inside. The outer senses are silent in such transitional states of mind, but what is in the inner soul life becomes active. When the outer senses are silent, the inner senses come alive.

We have three parts of the soul: the sentient or feeling soul, the rational soul and the consciousness soul. Just as eyes and ears have different relationships to the outer world, these three parts of the human soul have different relationships to the outer world.

(Here we pause to read Rudolf Steiner's definitions of these parts of the soul from his book, *Theosophy*, 1904.)

1. The "sentient soul or feeling soul" is part of the human soul being. To these sentients or feelings connect the feelings of lust, non-lust, the drives or desires, the instincts, and the passions. All of these have the same character of individual life as the feelings. Like the feelings they are dependent on the physical body. As is the case with the body, the feeling soul interacts with thinking and with the spirit. Thinking uses this part of the soul when the person builds thoughts about his feelings.

2. Through the feeling soul, the human being is related to animals. We notice that animals also have feelings, desires, instincts, and passions. But the animal follows these immediately. The animal will not weave independent thoughts into the immediate experience. This is also true, to some extent, of less developed human beings. The pure feeling soul is therefore different from the developed, higher part of the soul which thinking serves. The part of the soul that uses thinking is called the "rational soul." The rational soul transcends the feeling soul.

3. As far as the human being allows independent truth and goodness to live in his inner life, he raises himself above the feeling soul. The eternal spirit shines within. An eternal light is lit. So long as the human soul lives in this light, it partakes in the eternal. The soul unites the eternal with its own being. What the soul carries within as truth and goodness is eternal in it. That which enlightens in the eternal in the human soul is called the "consciousness soul." With the idea of

consciousness we can speak of the lower soul regions. The daily feelings are the objects of our consciousness. In this way the animals also have consciousness. The core of human consciousness, the soul within the soul, is considered the "consciousness soul." The rational soul is still caught in the feelings, desires and instincts, etc. Everyone knows what he feels is true. The truth remains after it has been removed from the aftertaste of the sympathy and antipathy within the feelings. The truth is true, even when all of the personal feelings are against it. The part of the soul in which these truths live is called the consciousness soul.

In that way people in such clairvoyant, transitional states of mind may observe according to which part of their soul is directed to a certain part of the spiritual world. For example, if the feeling soul observes a certain spiritual area, then the human being sees the spiritual beings that are closely related to forces of nature to the elements of nature. He does not see the mirror of these natural forces, but he sees what lives in the mirror of the natural forces of wind and water and in other processes. The person using his feeling soul sees the beings that express themselves in natural forces. Within these experiences he lives in a time before human beings used their rational soul or their consciousness soul.

The human is then placed in a setting as he observed in ancient times without his rational soul or his consciousness soul. But in ancient times he was closely related to the forces of nature. He was part of them. He was a being with a physical body, an etheric body, an astral body and a feeling soul.

He could act as the lower forces of nature act today. In roaring windstorms he could bring down trees. He could control weather, clouds and rain. In his ancient clairvoyance the powerful beings appeared, that were somewhat like himself at an earlier stage when mankind had not yet removed the forces of nature from their beings. The shapes that appeared were representations of their human shape, they appeared as people with gigantic powers. Those were the "giants"! In such clairvoyant, transitional states of mind, they saw giants as real figures that represented human beings with gigantic powers. But giants are stupid. They appear from a time in which they could not use their rational soul. They are strong and stupid.

Now let us look at what the rational soul can view when it is in such a transitional state of mind. It can see how everything is formed according to certain wisdom, not through brute power as with the giants. When the human being is living in the rational soul, he observes beings and forms that bring wisdom into play. While the giants appear as males, the forms of the rational soul appear as female beings. They are the "wise women" that form everything. In this form the human being sees his own form, for he does not yet have a consciousness soul. He feels: What I see in these wise, female beings is deeply connected to me. Therefore we often hear in fairy tales the "sister-motif" when these female beings appear.

And when the human being lives in his consciousness soul he experiences something in his soul that he can grasp very intimately. When his state of mind is somewhere beyond the normal, physical observations, he says to himself: What I see there is something that is contained in my daily observations in the rational soul, but when I see it by day, it is just the opposite. When the person is in the transitional state of mind and remembers his daily impressions, they appear as the opposite of what he felt when he remembers during his daily consciousness how the transitional state of mind appeared. They are scampering forms in his astral system. When he remembers his daily impressions, they appear as fine, etheric forms presented in stiff shapes behind normal reality. Therefore the daily objects appear as though enchanted in their being. Wherever forms appear that are enchanted, in plants or anywhere else, it takes place because the human being experiences the content of a wise being behind the physical appearance and he remembers: By day that is merely a plant, and it is separate from my rational soul so I may not reach it in my daily consciousness. When the human feels this strangeness between the daily objects and those objects behind them, for example the lily, and the being behind it, the form that is related to the rational soul, then he wants to unite his rational soul with that being. It is like a marriage, a growing together of a day-form with a night-form.

The consciousness soul appeared in human beings at a time when he had distanced himself from natural forces. He could no longer observe the secrets of the being. That is far, far away from the consciousness soul. Smartness is the key ability of the consciousness soul but this part of the soul is far away from strength, from great power. With the consciousness soul we observe the spiritual beings that have remained at the level of the human being when he had the first sheaths of his Self or I. The human being sees these beings but they are weak and not capable of much. And when a human being views the spiritual beings that are related to his own being, he observes them as "dwarfs."

The kingdom that lies beyond our sensory observations in daily life is filled with forms, as I have expressed. And when the human being is smart in his daily life, when he does not look dryly and unimaginatively at life but awakens to the spiritual realties, especially in the transitional states of mind, then the following can happen to him.

Imagine that a levelheaded person observes how smart some people are. He sees how they have overcome the raw forces that otherwise rage in human beings. This person says to himself: What actually takes place in life, where cleverness overcomes the raw forces, is due to powers beyond the physical world. They create in us an awareness of how our intelligence overcomes raw forces that we had inside ourselves as we were at the level of the giants. The happenings in his inner life appear as mirror images of outer realities in the world that have receded, but remain in the spiritual world.

In the spiritual world the battles between those beings that are weaker in bodies and stronger in their spiritual power are mirrored. Whenever the raw forces are overcome or a giant appears in a fairy tale, this is the basis for the observation in a transitional state of mind. The human being is trying to become more enlightened about himself. The spiritual world is no longer visible but he says: I can enlighten myself when I am in transitional states of mind. Then I am wise and cleverness has overcome the raw forces. The battle is won! And the powers appear that are in the spiritual world that correspond to our cleverness and smartness. They appear, act and enlighten human beings about what takes place in the spiritual world.

The human being says: What I have seen and spoken happened once. But in truth it happens continually in the spiritual world beyond the physical, sensory world where we live. The occurrences are not here nor there but wherever someone is able to observe them. Therefore the fairy tales must always begin:

Something happened once. Yes, where did it happen? Well, where did it not happen? That is the correct beginning to a fairy tale. And every fairy tale must end with: I once saw that; and if those happenings (in the spiritual world) have not ended, then they live on today. When you tell fairy tales, you create the right feeling if you begin and end in this way.

Imagine that someone searched for a bride as the King does in the second fairy tale. He is searching for a being that is represented in the human world as exactly as possible. It is the archetype of the human being that may be found in the spiritual world. It may be found in the wise activities of the forces that may be perceived through the rational soul. In our daily life these beings may not be found. Therefore he must subject the outer human being to the more intimate human being. In the physical world the human being is subject to error. He must allow the deeper forces to prevail when he wants to discover something of this nature. He can do this, even today, when he is in the transitional state of mind and places himself in relation to those prevailing forces. However, the people that carry such forces live in hiding where they will not be distracted by the major activities in the world. Therefore the King must go to his friend, the hermit who lives simply in poverty, but knows the secret of the forces that connect human beings to the spiritual world. Only his friend can give him the rosemary branch.

In the daily, outer world the King may not find something that must be decided by his archetypal pictures in the spiritual world. Therefore he dreams at first that a golden bird comes to him. He remains in the dreamlike, but awakened state of mind. And there he feels his way into the spiritual world where everything takes place in the fairy tale I told. Eventually he meets the forces that oppose human dignity and purity from which he learns the possibility for pure joy in human beings, joy that is still available today. Once again these forces do not appear from the physical world but are available when the rational soul is directed with inner soul forces to the spiritual world. This appears in the image of the magic horse. The horse we see in the physical world is merely a mirror image of the spiritual reality that lies behind it. The destructive soul forces in the physical world that are embodied in the physical world have driven the arrow into the body of the horse. However; in the moment when these forces are driven out, when the magic horse is liberated, the forces become active that allow the King to judge so he not only perceives in the outer world but also can find what is truly right for him. With his normal rationality he could look in the physical world for the wife who is suited for him but he would not see her. He would not understand the forces that prevent him from finding her and his previous conditions would continue.

The conditions he is looking for are there but they are not available in the physical world where everything appears changed. Within the physical world we do not have the forces in their true reality. But in the enchanted Glass King appears the true personality who can guide him to where he should look for his wife. Through the opposing forces in the physical world, the Glass King has just been transformed. He is caught in the outer, worldly conditions. This also changed him inwardly. Human beings have realities in their karma that are not right. The king has a reality that disturbs him—the bumblebee in his stomach.

The images or pictures in the tale display the truth that lies beneath the surface. In the whole situation we imagine how the forces that can find the spiritual reality beyond the physical world become active in the King. When his soul forces are engaged and he directs them properly, then the King finds what is hidden for him in the physical world: his wife.

This was possible because he came in contact with the hermit who could show him the way to engage deeper forces within. In this way a person may be guided to the forces that at first appear as untrue in the physical world but that he needs if he shall perceive and understand the truth. We see how outer situations influence us but that other states of consciousness are also available that create true perception.

Every fairy tale may be interpreted in this way, but they must be interpreted out of the entire spiritual reality behind the world of fairy tales. Everything we find in fairy tales, even the most minute details, may be interpreted. For example, the secretive connection between the observable forces and the secretive forces in daily life can become visible when you look inwardly. These are wonderfully symbolized in the meeting between the rosemary branch and the lily. Within the lily rest very fine, higher spiritual forces, but they must be touched by the rosemary branch. Only then will they appear.

The established belief in the world of fairy tales entails that we are surrounded by an enchanted spiritual reality and the human being reaches truth when he disenchants the enchanted spiritual world. In as far as the fairy tales are collected from the words of the local people, we have the remains of an ancient picture viewed in the astral world, but some details may be changed. Then the interpreter can easily make the mistake of interpreting the added details, especially in a spiritual direction. Yet in a real interpretation of a fairy tale you must return to the original form and understand it.

We can ask ourselves whether the human being had the same form as he has today at the time when his experiences in the transformed state of mind took place. No, he did not. The human being has gone through changes in his form until he has developed the form he now has. The human being had to remove the giant forces from his form. He had to overcome those forces and create finer forces in order to reach the level of the rational soul and the consciousness soul. There are beings that remained on the level where raw forces remained. Wherever the human being sees something as bad, something that must be overcome on the astral plane, it appears as a "dragon" or as similar things that are nothing more than grotesque, untransformed forms that the human being removed from his being and left behind in the spiritual world.

To end the lecture I would like to share a tale that you can work on further. It has multiple motifs that are played out when the human being enters into a relationship with the spiritual world. The motifs appear united within himself. And when you put everything we just interpreted into this complicated fairy tale, the paths will appear by themselves. This fairy tale is a synthesis, a summary of the most varied forces that play into each other.

Something happened once. Yes, where did it happen? Well, it could have happened everywhere. Where did it not happen? An old King lived. He had three sons and three daughters. As he began to die, the King said to his three sons: "Give the three daughters to the first people who stop by, so they do not remain unmarried. That is the first instruction that I want to give you. The second is that you should not go to a certain place, especially not in the night." And he showed them the place underneath a poplar tree in the forest.

After the King died his sons tried to follow his instructions. The very first evening something yelled into the window that they should give it one of the King's daughters. The brothers did so and threw their sister out of the window. On the second evening something yelled into the window that they should give it one of the King's daughters. The brothers threw the second daughter out of the window. And on the third evening something yelled into the window that they should give it also one of the King's daughters, and the brothers threw their third sister out of the window. Now they were all alone.

But the brothers became curious and wanted to know how to explain the poplar tree. One evening they went out, sat down below the poplar tree, made a bonfire and went to sleep. The eldest brother kept watch. As he walked back and forth carrying his sword, he saw something that started eating the bonfire. When he looked closer he saw a three-headed dragon. He started a fight with the dragon. The brother won the battle, buried the dragon, but did not tell his brothers what had happened. In the morning they all walked home.

The next evening they went out again. Once again they made a fire and lay down to sleep. This time the second brother should keep watch. Soon he saw something eating the fire, and when he came closer he saw a six-headed dragon. The second brother fought the six-headed dragon and won. After burying the dragon he decided not to tell his brothers about the battle, and so the other brothers thought nothing had happened. That morning they returned to their house.

On the third evening they made another fire, and this time the youngest brother held watch. The others had just gone to sleep when he walked back and forth with his sword and saw something eating the fire. He looked closer but was hesitant and took his time to react. Then he began a sword fight with the nine-headed dragon. Just as he won the battle, the fire went out. He did not want to surprise his brothers so he walked into the woods to look for light. Between the branches he saw some light that he wanted to grab, but it was too little. He saw something fighting in the air and asked what it was. The fighting beings answered, "We are the sun and the sunrise. We are fighting for the day."

He took off his belt and bound the sun and the sunrise together so the day could not begin. He walked on to find light and fire. The boy arrived at a campfire where three giants were asleep. He helped himself to some fire but when he tried to step over one of the giants, some of the fire fell on the giant and he awoke. With one hand he grabbed the boy, lifted him up and said to the others, "Look at the mosquito I have caught!" The King's son was extremely unhappy, for the giants wanted to kill him. But before they killed him they wanted something and therefore they made an agreement. They wanted to have three King's daughters but a dog and a chicken made such a terrible noise that they could not get in. The King's son promised to help them; therefore they set him free.

They tied him to thin thread and let him walk off. They agreed that every time he pulled on the thread, one of the giants would come to him. He soon arrived at a stream which he could not cross. His brothers were still asleep. The boy pulled on the thread, a giant came along and threw a huge tree trunk across the river so he could travel on.

Later he arrived at the King's castle where his three sisters should have been. He entered and found one sister in her room. She lay on a copper bed and had a golden ring on her finger. He removed the golden ring from her hand, put it on his and walked on.

He entered the second room where the sister lay on a silver bed with a golden ring on her finger as well. He removed it and put it on his finger. The boy entered the third room where his third sister lay on a golden bed with a golden ring on her finger and as with the others he put her ring on his hand.

When he looked around the castle, he found an entrance with a very small opening. He pulled on the thread and a giant came. In that very moment when the giant put his head through the door, the boy cut it off with his sword. To the second and third giants he did the same. Now he had killed all three giants. After releasing the sun and the sunrise, he returned to his brothers. They looked at each other and said, "Oh, that was a long night." They looked at their youngest brother but he told nothing of his adventures. They all walked home.

After a while all three boys wanted to get married. The third brother said he knew where three King's daughters lived and led them to the castle. The King's sons married all three daughters. The youngest married the most beautiful daughter who lay on the golden bed. He become the heir to his father-in-law and must therefore stay in the foreign land.

After a while he wanted to visit his homeland and take his wife with him, but the King warned him, "When you return to your homeland, you will lose your wife at the border and probably never see her again!"

Despite his warning they wanted to travel, so travel they did. To be more secure they took three giants along with them. As they crossed the border his wife was overcome by a secret power that carried her away. He returned to his father-in-law and asked him where and how he could find his wife. The King replied, "If there is any chance at all, you can only find her in the white land."

The King's son traveled far to find his wife. Yet he did not know the way to the white land. He came to a castle and decided to ask where was the path that led to the white land. As he entered the castle, he saw the wife of the castle sitting on her throne. When he saw her, he immediately knew she was one of his sisters, whom his brothers had thrown out of the window. He asked her where to look for his wife.

Something cried from another hall and a four-headed dragon appeared. The boy asked him where to look for his wife. The dragon said he did not know where the white land is but that possibly the animals may know. The animals were called in but none of them knew where the path to the white land could be found.

The King's son walked on and eventually came to a second castle. Here he found his second sister that his brothers had thrown out of the window. He asked for his wife, but no one knew where she was. They called in an eight-headed dragon and asked him where she may be. The dragon knew nothing of the white land, but perhaps the animals may know, so they called in all the animals, but none of them knew the way.

The King's son was forced to travel on. After a while he found a third castle. There he entered and found his third sister. He told her what he wanted but she answered very sadly. Her husband was called for and a twelve-headed dragon entered. They asked him how to find the white land. He said he did not know, but maybe the animals knew.

So all the animals were called in. Among them was a lame wolf. He spoke, "Once I entered a white land by mistake. It was strange, for now I am lame. I know the white land. Unfortunately, I know it! The King's son told the wolf that he wanted to be led into the white land. But the wolf did not want to, not even if he were promised a shepherd's whole flock of lambs. Yet the wolf eventually agreed to lead him to the nearby mountain where they both stood and looked down into the white land. There the lame wolf left him on his own.

The King's son found a spring. He drank from it and felt wonderfully refreshed from the water. A woman approached him and he immediately recognized his stolen wife. She knew him too, stating, "You may not take me back. If you did, the magician who is now my husband would take me away on his magic horse that can fly through the air as fast as a thought!

The King's son asked, "Yes, then what should we do?"

And she replied, "There is one way, but we will need an even faster horse. Go to the old woman who lives on the border to this land. You must work for her as her servant. She will give you very difficult trials, but you must find a way to survive. As a reward you shall ask for the youngest colt and the saddle on the floor that is covered with chicken manure. Ask her for the bridle as well!"

With these instructions the King's son went forth. He came to a little brook. As he rested there he saw on the edge of the brook a fish lying on the ground. The fish begged him, "Take me and throw me back in the water. You will do a great deed!" He did so, and as he leaned down to pick it up, the fish gave him a whistle and said, "If you need anything take the whistle, blow in it and I will be at your service." He put the whistle in his pocket and placed the fish back in the brook.

After a short while he met an ant who was being followed by her enemy, the spider. He freed the ant, who gave him a second whistle that he could play anytime to call her to his service. He placed it in another pocket and walked on.

Soon he met a fox who had been wounded by a silver arrow in his body. The wolf challenged him, "If you pull the arrow out of my body and give me some sharp-pointed herbs for my wound, you will be helped when entering a dangerous experience." The King's son did so and the fox gave him a third whistle.

With three whistles in his pocket, the boy reached the border to the white land where the old woman lived. He told her he wanted to be her servant. She agreed to let him try, but told him that no one had succeeded with the terribly hard work she demanded. She took him out to the fields. There were ninety-nine people sleeping there. The oldest spoke, "Here are all the people who tried to be her servant but none of them has succeeded. You may try but if you are unsuccessful, you will be the one-hundredth!" He agreed to serve her for one year, but in this land one year was only three days.

On the first day the old woman cooked for him a "dream soup" and then she sent him out with three horses. He had drunk the "dream soup" and went to sleep immediately. When he awoke all three horses were gone. He remembered his whistles, pulled one out and blew into it. Nearby there was a well. Three goldfish swam to the surface. As he touched them they transformed into three horses. He brought the horses the old woman. It was she who had transformed the horses into goldfish, and when she saw the horses, she cursed the boy and tossed herself from one side to another.

The next day the old woman cooked another "dream soup" and sent him off with the horses. Once again he fell asleep and when he awoke the horses were gone. He blew into the second whistle and immediately three golden ants appeared. As he touched them they were transformed into his three horses again. He led them back to the old woman. She went totally wild! She had enchanted them and now cursed them even more. But the King's son was saved.

On the third day the old lady said to herself, "Now things have to be done even more cleverly!" She cooked another soup and sent him out with the horses. When he fell asleep from the dream soup, the horses were transformed into three eggs.

Then the old woman placed them under her buttocks and sat on them! When the King's son awoke, the horses were gone. He blew into the third whistle and just imagine how clever things took place. The fox came by and said, "This time things are much more difficult, but we will figure it out. I will go to the henhouse and cause wild noise and chaos. The old lady will run out. While she runs, take the three eggs she is sitting on and they will be transformed the minute you touch them."

So it came to pass. The fox entered the chicken coop, stirred up a ruckus, and when the old woman ran out, the King's son touched the golden eggs one by one. When the old lady came back, all three horses were there again. She could do nothing more than ask the boy: "What do you want as a reward?" She thought he would want something very special. He asked for the colt that was born that morning and the saddle on the floor that was covered by chicken manure and the old bridle. He received all of these and went along his way.

The horse was very small. He had to carry it on his back. That evening the colt said, "Now you can sleep a bit. I will go to the well and drink some water." In the morning the colt returned. On the second day the colt could run at tremendous speeds. And on the third day it carried the King's son to the place where his wife was banished. He placed his wife on the colt (and this is the point that proves to anyone who understands these things the occult origin of fairy tales), and the King's son asked, "How fast shall we fly through the air?"

And his wife answered, "With the speed of thought."

Now when the magician who had imprisoned her saw they were escaping, he mounted his magic horse to hurry after them. The horse asked him, "How fast shall we fly through the air?"

And he answered, "With the speed of will or the speed of thinking!" And they rushed after them, getting nearer and nearer. When they were quite near, the horse told those who flew ahead to stop.

"I will stop only when you are quite close," was the answer.

In that moment the magic horse reared, threw off the robber and joined the little colt. So the Queen was freed, the King's son was able to go home with his wife, and they lived again in their own land.

And if what happened did not fade away, then they must still live on today.

⁕

This is a much more complicated fairy tale that contains multiple events. Let us allow this tale to live in us in order to let the events in this tale resound together. Then we can interpret it on our own. Whatever has been included from false traditions must be extracted. If you follow the principles I have explained today, you will find the golden thread: the dragon motif, the motif of three sisters, the banishment, the overcoming of dragon forces by the fires, the motif of cleverness, the motif of marriage between the rational soul and the outer world; then once again the unique motif of cleverness within the finer magical forces. Then there appears, in a strange fashion, nemesis, karma, in that the King's son meets his sisters again: their higher sisterly nature that three brothers threw out the window, killing the dragons by the fires and so forth.

Such fairy tales are experiences from people within a folk who are in transformative, in-between states of mind. In the same way we have received the great mythologies of the gods from different peoples. Initiates have brought these mythologies to us from the higher and the lower spiritual worlds. The fairy tales relate to the great folk mythologies in the following way: The great folk mythologies can be interpreted when we base them upon the great, all-encompassing conditions of the cosmos.

The fairy tales are interpreted when based upon the secrets of a folk. Everything that appears in fairy tales is nothing other than different events and pictures of storytelling from the lower spiritual world. To a certain degree all people in primeval times had such experiences from the lower spiritual world. Then they happened more and more seldom. One person told another. Others received the tales and they were transported from one area to the next. They appeared in different languages so we notice common fairy tale treasures over the entire earth when we can peel away the experiences, they are based upon, from the lower spiritual world.

Any practical person who wanders upon the earth can find the final remains of atavistic clairvoyance. From time to time we meet someone who speaks about experiences he had in the lower spiritual worlds. Such a person, who wanders through the country, hears from others who have an understanding for the true reality of fairy tales. In this way the Brothers Grimm wrote down the German fairy tales. Others have collected their land's fairy tales; most of whom were not clairvoyant, but collected tales from third, fourth, fifth hand and sometimes from tenth hand so the tales take on a multi-distorted form. Yet the fading light of twilight is approaching when people had an intimate relationship to the spiritual world. More and more people return from this spiritual world. The atavistic clairvoyance will become more and more seldom. At least that can be considered healthy. And true clairvoyance will be more and more accessible for people as the result of spiritual development.

And concerning those who saw in primeval times, people in the future will be able to say, "Once upon a time ancient people spoke from their experiences in the lower spiritual worlds. Where was it? It can be everywhere."

Today we seldom find someone who can speak out of the true source of fairy tales experiences. For most people who are inwardly trapped in the physical world, the tales died a long time ago. But from the fairy tale experiences we can say, "They happened once—and if they are not finished, then these fairy tale experiences are still alive today."

50 *Interpreting Fairy Tales*

REFERENCES:

Steiner, Rudolf. *Die Beantwortung von Welt- und Lebensfragen durch Anthroposophie*, "Interpreting Fairy Tales," Lecture in Berlin, December 26, 1908, Rudolf Steiner Verlag in Dornach, Switzerland 1986, GA 108, pp. 143–168.

_____. *Theosophy*, First Edition in Berlin 1904, Rudolf Steiner Verlag Edition in Dornach, Switzerland 1976, GA 9, pp. 34–38.

_____. *Anthroposophy and the Human Gemüt*, September 1923, Vienna.

How to Create, Tell, and Recall a Story

by Rudolf Steiner
translated by Helen Fox

Let me give you an example of something which can sink into the child's soul so that it grows with his growth, something which one can come back to in later years and make use of to arouse certain feelings within him. Nothing is more useful and fruitful in teaching than to give the children something in picture form between the seventh and eighth years, and later, perhaps in the fourteenth and fifteenth years, come back to again in some way or other. Just for this reason we try to let the children in the Waldorf school remain as long as possible with one teacher. When they come to school at seven years of age, the children are given over to a teacher who then takes his class up the school as far as he can, for it is good that things which at one time were given to the child in germ can again and again furnish the content of the methods employed in his education.

Now suppose for instance that we tell an imaginative story to a child of seven or eight. He does not need to understand all at once the pictures which the story contains; why that is, I will explain later. All that matters is that the child takes delight in the story because it is presented with a certain grace and charm. Suppose I were to tell the following story:

⇒》《⇐

Once upon a time in a wood where the sun peeped through the branches, there lived a very modest violet under a tree with big leaves. And the violet was able to look through an opening at the top of the tree. As she looked through this broad opening in the treetop, the violet saw the blue sky. The little violet saw the blue sky for the first time on this morning because she had only just blossomed. Now the violet was frightened when she saw the blue sky—indeed, she was overcome with fear, but she did not yet know why she felt such great fear. Then a dog ran by, not a good dog, a rather bad snappy dog. And the violet said to the dog: "Tell me, what is that up there that is blue like me?" For the sky was blue just as the violet was.

And the dog in his wickedness said: "Oh, that is a great giant violet like you and this great violet has grown so big that it can crush you." Then the violet was more frightened than ever because she believed that the violet up in the sky was so big that it could crush her. And the violet folded her little petals together and did not want to look up to the great big violet anymore, but hid herself under a big leaf which a puff of wind had just blown down from the tree. There she stayed all day long, hiding in fear from the great big sky-violet.

When morning came the violet had not slept at all, for she had spent the night wondering what to think of the great blue sky-violet who was said to be coming to crush her. And every moment she was expecting the first blow to come. But it did not come. In the morning the little violet crept out, as she was not in the least bit tired. For all night long she had been only thinking, and she was fresh and not tired (violets are tired when they sleep, they are not tired when they don't sleep!) and the first thing that the little violet saw was the rising sun and the rosy dawn. And when the violet saw the rosy dawn, she had no fear. She was glad at heart and happy to see the dawn. As the dawn faded, the pale blue sky gradually appeared again and became bluer and bluer all the time, and the little violet thought again of what the dog had said, that this was a great big violet which would come and crush her.

At that moment a lamb came by and the little violet again felt she must ask what that thing above her could be. "What is that up there?" asked the violet.

And the lamb said, "That is a great big violet, blue like yourself." Then the violet was afraid again and thought she would hear from the lamb just what the wicked dog had told her.

But the lamb was good and gentle, and because he had such good, gentle eyes, the violet asked again: "Dear lamb, do tell me, will the great big violet up there come and crush me?"

"Oh, no," answered the lamb. "It will not crush you. It is a great big violet, and his love is much greater than your own love, even as he is much more blue than you are in your little blue form." And the violet understood at once that there was a great big violet who would not crush her, but who was so blue in order that he might have more love, and that the big violet would protect the little violet from everything in the world which might hurt her.

Then the little violet felt so happy because what she saw as blue in the great sky-violet appeared to her as Divine Love, which was streaming towards her from all sides. And the little violet looked up all the time as if she wished to pray to the God of violets.

⇾⇢⇠⇽

Now, if you tell the children a story of this kind, they will most certainly listen, for they always listen to such things. But you must tell it in the right mood so that when the children have listened to the story, they somehow feel the need to live with it and turn it over inwardly in their souls. This is very important, and it all depends on whether the teacher is able to keep discipline in the class through his own feeling.

That is why when we speak of such things as I have just mentioned, we must also consider this question of keeping discipline. We once had a teacher in the Waldorf school, who could tell the most wonderful stories, but he did not make such an impression upon the children that they looked up to him with unquestioned love. What was the result? When the first thrilling story had been told, the children immediately want another. The teacher yielded to this wish and prepared a second. Then they immediately wanted a third, and the teacher gave in again and prepared a third story for them. And at last it came about that after a time this teacher simply could not prepare enough stories. But we must not be continually pumping into the children like a steam pump; there must be a variation, as we shall hear in a moment, for now we must go further and let the children ask questions. We should be able to see from the face and gestures of a child that he wants to ask a question. We let him ask it, and then talk it over with him in connection with the story that has just been related.

Thus a little child might ask: "But why did the dog give such a horrid answer?" and then in a simple childlike way you will be able to show him that a dog is a creature whose task is to watch, who has to bring fear to people, who is accustomed to make people afraid of him, and you will be able to explain why the dog gave that answer.

You can also explain to the children why the lamb gave the answer that he did. After telling the story, you can go on talking to the children like this for some time. Then you will find that one question leads to another, and eventually the children will bring up every imaginable kind of question.

Your task in all this is really to bring into the class the unquestioned authority about which we have still much to say. Otherwise it will happen that while you are speaking to one child, the others will begin to play pranks and be up to all sorts of mischief. And if you are then forced to turn around and give a reprimand, you are lost! Especially with the little children one must have the gift of letting a great many things pass unnoticed.

But now let us consider the following question: Why did I choose a story with this particular content? It was because the thought-pictures which are given in this story can grow with the child. You have all kinds of things in the story which you can come back to later. The violet is afraid because she sees the great big violet above her in the sky. You need not yet explain this to the little child, but later when you are dealing with more complicated teaching matter, and the question of fear comes up, you can recall this story. Things small and great are contained in this story, for indeed things small and great are repeatedly coming up again in life and working upon each other. Later on then you can come back to this. The chief feature of the early part of the story is the snappish advice given by the dog, and later on it is the kind, loving words of advice uttered by the lamb. And when the child has come to treasure these things in his heart and has grown older, how easily then you can lead on from the story you told him before to thoughts about good and evil, and about such contrasting feelings which are rooted in the human soul. And even with a much older pupil, you can go back to this simple child's story; you can make it clear to him that we are often afraid of things simply because we misunderstand them and because they have been presented to us wrongly. This cleavage in the feeling life, which may be spoken of later in connection with this or that lesson, can be demonstrated in the most wonderful way if you come back to the story in the later school years.

In the religion lessons too, which will come later on, how well this story can be used to show how the child develops religious feelings through what is great, for the great is the protector of the small, and one must develop true religious feeling by finding in oneself those elements of greatness which have a protective impulse. The little violet is a little blue being. The sky is a great blue being, and therefore the sky is the great blue God of the violet.

This concept can be used at various different stages in the religion lessons. What a beautiful analogy one can draw later on by showing how the human heart itself is of God. One can then say to the child: "Look, this great sky-violet, the God of the violets, is all blue and stretches out in all directions. Now think of a little bit cut out of it—that is the little violet. So God is as great as the world-ocean. Your soul is a drop in this ocean of God. But as the water of the sea, when it forms a drop, is the same water as the great sea, so your soul is the same as the great God is; only it is just a little drop of it."

If you find the right pictures you can work with the child in this way all through the early years, for you can come back to these pictures again when the child is more mature. But the teacher himself must find pleasure in this picture-making. And you will see that when, by your won powers of invention, you have worked out a dozen of these stories, then you simply cannot escape them; they come rushing in upon you wherever you may be. For the human soul is like an inexhaustible spring that can pour out its treasures unceasingly as soon as the first impulse has been called forth. But often people are so indolent that they will not make the initial effort to bring forth what is in their souls.

RESOURCE:
Translated by Helen Fox and printed as lecture four in *The Kingdom of Childhood*, Rudolf Steiner Press, London, 1974. In German the lecture is found in GA 311, *Die Kunst des Erziehens aus dem Erfassen der Menschenwesenheit.*

The Secret of Children's Pictures

by Armin Krenz
translated by Nina Kuettel

For many decades scientists from all over the world have tried to decipher the meaning behind human beings' pictorial art. They have found that children's pictures, especially, have commonalities that transcend culture. These commonalities include the experiences represented, as well as the forms of their expression. The consistencies are so pervasive that it can be no coincidence when children just draw "something or other."

No matter if a child paints something quickly in passing or makes a big effort, whether the best colored pencil is carefully chosen, or the first one that comes to hand is used, if one investigates the "meaning" of children's pictures, it can be established that children always express their hopes, wishes, dreams, visions, and expectations, and also their anxieties, fears, hurts, and cares with their pictures. The pictures portray their current, experienced reality; an experience in the present that has a connection to the past and the future. Of course, children's pictures are not conscious acts of creation. That is why developmental psychologists do not say: "The child is painting," but rather, "painting has overtaken the child." By "overtaken" they are referring to the feelings and internal pictures that play into the painting process.

The "purpose" of children's pictures simply lies in the joy the children have in painting and drawing and their desire for "self expression." Self expression connotes wanting to bring out something that is pressing on one. This feeling of pressure should not be compared to a burdensome experience! It is much more that a person's desire to free himself of feelings or thoughts in order to be open to new perceptions and experiences gives rise to this sort of pressure. One could say: Children's pictures enhance and free them from feelings, relieve them from unassimilated thoughts and concerns, so there is the possibility of moving forward in life's present situations.

A principle of developmental psychology helps us understand something that is of the highest importance in children's painting and drawing: There is no "right or wrong," "good or bad," "acceptable or unacceptable," "pretty or less pretty" in the pictorial-graphic expressions of children! When children subjectively appraise and evaluate themselves and their whole environment, that is, judge with value measurements that are coated in emotion, then their pictures always equal their own idea of rightness. It is not without reason that in neurobiology it is said: How a person feels is how they think, and how they think is how they act. Emotions are impressed upon our thoughts and influence their direction, releasing corresponding patterns of behavior. In this respect, there cannot and may not be any "objective correctness" applied to children's pictures!

When children paint and draw significant things especially large, then it may be that a lion will appear larger than a house or a tree. Their picture expressions give an emotion-laden image of their current assessment of their lives. In this respect, the picture is a stored bundle of impressions. And here, something cultural-historical comes full circle: Im-pression seeks out ex-pression. Children's pictures are equally ordered among the other five forms of expression.

How to "read" children's pictures

Children's pictures are composed of six major elements. First, there are the so-called twenty graphemes; the basic marks or scribbles that range from the dot, various vertical, diagonal, or horizontal lines, and curved, zigzag, or wavy lines, to the spiral and circle, all the way to open lines. Each grapheme corresponds to a certain phase of development in the first four years of a child's life. How often a certain grapheme is chosen can be concluded from the particular developmental focus at the time.

Secondly, we look at the three personality elements: capacity for decision-making and responsibility, emotional capacity, and cognitive capacity. The pictures show us how strongly each particular area is developed or not. In the third step the elements of time are considered: past, present, and future. The pictures inform us as to what aspect of time the child is most strongly living in with respect to emotions and cognition.

58   *The Secret of Children's Pictures*

Of the many thousands of children's pictures that I have evaluated in the last twelve years, more than ninety percent lead me to the conclusion that children between the ages of four and seven grapple with family situations with intensively emotional thoughts that are drawn from the past. This observation is contrary to the cognitive, future-oriented learning methods promoted among many kindergarten-aged children at the present time. A radical change in perspective is necessary here in order to not further hinder a child's lasting personality development.

The fourth element involves the child's choice of color. Socio-cultural oriented educators place the highest priority of significance on the four primary and four secondary colors: Red, yellow, green and blue, as well as black, white, purple, and brown. These colors play a special role in human history and many current findings in developmental psychology show that children again and again attach the same colors to their emotionally packed experiences.

Girl, age five: Strong developmental orientation; is continuing to seek many possibilities for becoming more independent.

The boy who drew this picture was emotionally, socially and physically neglected by his parents. He desired a "world" in which he could "laugh and play."

Girl just under five years old: Self-aware, very autonomous – loves the freedom to actively take part in arranging the day and is discovering the world with its many possibilities for creating.

Now, in the fifth step, the finished picture is viewed, whereby a certain symbolic value is assigned, usually based on the work of Carl Gustav Jung. He worked from the assumption that every person comes into the world with an "enormous repository" of complete sets of pictures, drawings, and symbols in their subconscious mind that, through impressions and their assessment, are activated and networked with each other. Whether it is the sun, stars, the moon, clouds, a house, certain animals, a fence, a fire, a rainbow, a forest, an explosion, a mountain, or something else, here are archetypal pictures that have particular meanings.

Finally, specific characteristics are taken into consideration:
- Floating pictures in which people, animals, or objects have no floor or ground under their feet.
- Framed pictures in which the four sides of the page are outlined.
- Doubling of objects.
- The angle of incline for crowns of trees or roofs of houses.
- Leaving out parts or pieces of objects that belong together.
- Sealing or rolling up pictures.

Exercise caution in the analysis.

A conclusion about the interpretation of a picture is possible only under the following conditions:

- Several pictures must be available in order to discover the frequency of characteristics. Single pictures are seen as reflections of the day and would lead to haphazard generalizations.

- The basis for the work of analysis is verified knowledge.

- A complete conclusion is never achieved by evaluating single characteristics. It is the result of a combined look at all six focus points.

- Conclusions are only relevant if they concur with the analyses of the other five forms of expression. Children's pictures are extremely valuable documents in helping to understand the child's world, discover internal values and priorities, and convey educational measures. We should encounter all children's pictures with a sense of value and respect because they are entrusting to us the "diary of their soul."

The Secret of Children's Pictures

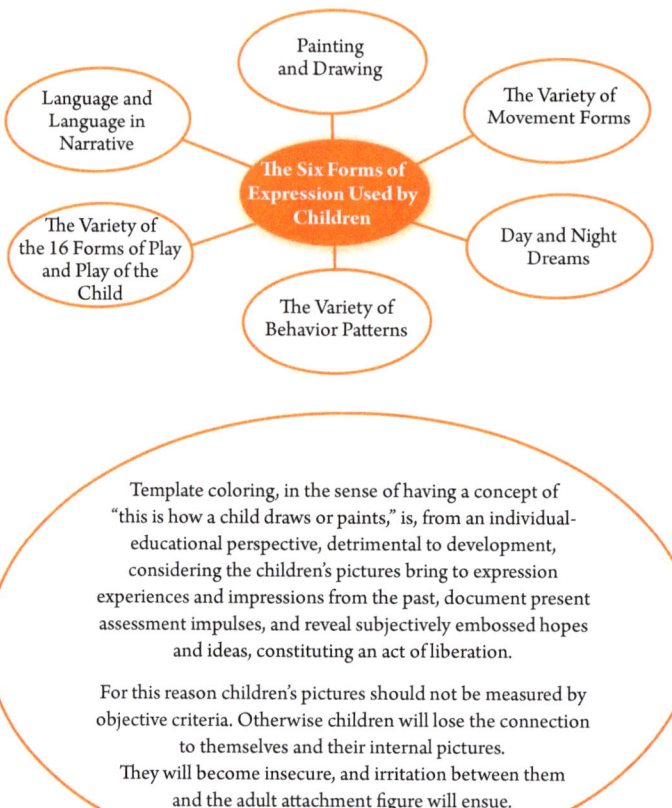

Template coloring, in the sense of having a concept of "this is how a child draws or paints," is, from an individual-educational perspective, detrimental to development, considering the children's pictures bring to expression experiences and impressions from the past, document present assessment impulses, and reveal subjectively embossed hopes and ideas, constituting an act of liberation.

For this reason children's pictures should not be measured by objective criteria. Otherwise children will lose the connection to themselves and their internal pictures. They will become insecure, and irritation between them and the adult attachment figure will ensue.

REFERENCES:

Armin Krenz: *Was Kinderzeichnungen erzählen. Kinder in ihrer Bildsprache verstehen,* Dortmund, 2010.

Hans-Günther Richter: *Die Kinderzeichnung, Entwicklung – Interpretation – Aesthetik,* Berlin, 1997.

Martin Schuster: *Kinderzeichnungen, Wie sie entstehen, was sie bedeuten,* Munich, 2010.

Wolfgang Sehringer: *Zeichnen und Malen als Instrumente der psychologischen Diagnostik, Ein Handbuch,* Heidelberg, 1999.

About the Author: Dr. Armin Krenz works for the Institut für angewandte Psychologie und Pädagogik (IFAP) Kiel with research and continuing education focus on professional developmental monitoring and quality in institutional elementary education.

Research into Resilience

by Christof Wiechert
translated and printed from *The Beating Drum: the South African Early Childhood Journal out of the Rudolf Steiner Impulse*

Disturbing reports are circulating around the world, always in the murky twilight of so-called 'facts.' According to the rumors, or indeed facts, that we are dealing with, a disproportionate number of war veterans commit suicide on their return to the USA from their tour in Iraq. After the Vietnam War, accounts came in from various sides of how soldiers were able to cope again with everyday civilian life only with great effort. People in Europe are also worried about the NATO soldiers' ability to deal with trauma when they are in peace-keeping missions abroad. The question is, How does an individual cope with traumatic or otherwise shattering events in his or her life? This question is just as valid for children as for adults.

The research that deals with this is research into resilience—research into the overcoming, the processing of, 'insurmountable' experiences, research into the sours (mental) power of resistance (*resilire* = to spring back, to rebound).

This research began after World War II, when people were faced with the fact that there were those who inwardly overcame their experiences of war or prison and were able to resume a 'normal' life once their soul wounds were healed. At the same time, they realized there were those who never really overcame these experiences and instead kept suffering from the trauma affecting them.

The question arose on what this ability to inwardly overcome experiences depends. What makes one child strong in taking life's knocks, what makes another child react so much more sensitively? From regions where people have been hit by great natural disasters, we hear relatively little of the problems that they have in inwardly coming to terms with them.

Research into resilience has arrived at several conclusions that have considerable significance for educators in particular. The first issue was to follow up on the question of whether the soul's power of resistance may be explained by heredity. If the parents have inner strength, is it passed on to their offspring? After numerous studies the conclusion was reached that this is not the case. Resilience is not inherited.

However, resilience is definitely connected with the experiences of the early years of childhood. One researcher thinks it is a matter of the first four or five years, while another thinks the whole time of childhood is significant, that is, until the tenth year. Leaving aside the different viewpoints, there is agreement that the soul's power of resistance, or resilience, is nurtured and developed, if children have had the following five experiences.

1. A reliable, stable relationship with one person. This person does not necessarily need to be the mother, but it is necessary for it to be a single person in the beginning. Later on this person may be joined by others. Neurologists also point out that at the start of life there must be only one person to relate to. Later on, there may be a second, followed by a third or fourth person, who is added to the circle of people the child relates to, but just not in the beginning.

2. The growing child needs the experience of an authoritative upbringing. This means that the child needs the fundamental experience that others (involved in its upbringing) decide for him/her, and that he/she is completely relieved of the necessity of making decisions, It is simply from the experience that others make the right decisions that the child gains a sense of security in life, in other words, trust. This experience cannot be estimated too highly. In the first place, others decide what is good or bad for me, what is right and wrong, healthy and unhealthy. A deep feeling of security comes about: I can leave it up to the world to take over; I can rely upon my surroundings in all circumstances.

3. Children need the experience of learning through example. This has to do with two qualities, firstly, a moral quality that makes a deep impression: What the child experiences through the example of the behavior of those around him should be completely compatible with what is demanded of him. If the child is forbidden to watch television and the people he relates to watch unlimited amounts of television, the child's understanding of his surroundings as a totality cracks open. You can add many other examples.

There is something else at stake too. When the Canadian psychologist Albert Bandura discovered the mirror neurons and their activity in human beings, the interesting question arose as to whether, in general, the child learns with his/her intellect or from imitation, from "doing it like this too." Bandura argues vehemently that the young child learns from imitating, not through cognition, something he documents impressively through the process of learning to speak.

To date, in the practice of teaching, this most significant idea, the idea that children learn in a more carefree way through imitation rather than laboriously drumming things into their heads, is scarcely to be found. In this case we are talking about children up to the age of ten. Through the process of a child's learning, for example, to do arithmetic by developing habits rather than through the intellect, self-confidence is developed as he learns 'externally'; he feels affirmed through the sure habit.

The research described here does not derive from an anthroposophical-anthropological milieu, but from conventional research. It is, therefore, legitimate to emphasize that, according to Steiner, from around the twelfth year cognitive learning takes on more and more significance. Only with Steiner is this whole complex called "becoming capable of forming judgments." In other words, the learning process is guided and determined by the child's own power of discrimination, no longer by habit.

4. Children need a qualitative experience of time. What is the difference between morning and evening for our feeling about life? What is the difference between autumn and spring, summer and winter for our feeling about life? Within a Christian context, how does the Easter festival differ from Christmas? Or within an Islamic context, how does the sugar festival differ from the beginning of Ramadan? How does the child experience the ordering of time, how do we help him to experience the ordering of time? Here is one quite simple example: when I was still quite young, people in Holland celebrated the Queen's birthday at the end of spring. This was the season when we used to visit the annual fair and celebrate the day we would be given cotton candy on a wooden stick. In our minds as children this cotton candy developed into the quintessence of the celebration of the Queen's birthday. Lots of biographies describe rituals that are linked to the seasons. There is also the simple fact of going to bed. Is it a random activity because we are tired, or is there a small ritual belonging to this moment when we take our leave of the day that is entirely different from waking up in the morning?

We can see from the way in which this fact is reflected in Waldorf kindergartens and schools that these festivals are not celebrated just for the sake of it, but rather out of some insight. Whoever wants to give shape to his or her life, whoever refuses to be 'lived' has to shape time.

5. The child needs a definite surplus of positive school experiences. The fifth condition from research into resilience scarcely requires an explanation, Nonetheless, it ought to be pointed out that for long periods of time (times which are not yet over) the question whether pupils are left with more positive than negative experiences from learning, from going to school, is considered incidental. This needs to be seen properly. Many school traumas will accompany the individual for his or her whole life, wounds of which the school (or the teachers) are often not aware. If they were aware of them, the schools would set things up differently. In other words, whatever basis is laid down for the mood of soul at school plays a key role in the memory of individuals for their lives. This is an important reason for schools and teachers to ask themselves how the pupils are faring. This is by no means to deny that school is a place where pupils can go through a crisis; this will also need to happen. What is at stake is the overcoming of difficulties and whether pupils feel sufficiently accepted by the teachers.

We will have no difficulty, after reading the above account, in establishing the basic requirements of the art of education. That is to say, the art of education is based on resilience. We are dealing with one aspect of resilience. Another aspect is concerned with the so-called education for dealing with emergencies. How do we help children who have survived natural disasters or war disasters? Nowadays, we know that what enables children to work through trauma more than anything else is art or artistic activity. (This can be gleaned from the Chengdu Waldorf school report.) This fact has been documented in lots of places and it confirms the healing power that can come from art. Art needs to become a normal part of every form of education.

REFERENCES:

Rutter, M. "Resilience Reconsidered," *Handbook of Early Child Intervention*, Cambridge University Press, 2000.

Steiner, R. *Die Pädagogische Praxis vom Gesichtspunkte der geisteswissenschaftlichen Menschen erkenntnis (GA 306)*, 5th Lecture, Dornach, 19th April 1923.

Werner, E. "Protective Factors and Individual Resilience," *Handbook of Early Childhood Intervention*, Cambridge University Press, 2000.

Resilient Children: First Food or Fast Food

by Kathrine Train
> nutritionist and psychophonetics practitioner in South Africa

printed from *The Beating Drum: The South African Early Childhood Journal out of the Rudolf Steiner Impulse*

Some of us are able to accommodate the stresses we're exposed to and continue life on an even keel; others are knocked off balance, which they express through their behavior or illness. Resilience is a term used to describe what it takes to remain on track.

Humanity today is exposed to a vast array of stressors on all levels—physical, electromagnetic and psychological. The environment has been manipulated by technology to such an extent that chemicals in food, water, households and the air are difficult to avoid. The use of electricity, radio, cell phones and internet determines that the air is congested with foreign electromagnetic and sound waves. On one level our bodies are made up of chemicals and waves, so this must be impacting us, not to mention the physical and emotional stress of conflict, trauma and just plain overdoing it that we inflict on ourselves and others on an ongoing basis.

We take experience into ourselves through sensing, food and the air that we breathe. Inside of ourselves, whether it is in the psyche or the body, we digest what we've brought in, make meaning of it and incorporate it into the sense of who we are. In this way we build ourselves up. There is a fine balance between challenging ourselves enough to grow, but not so much that we overwhelm ourselves. Resilient children have, through their experiences, developed a sense of self and bodily strength that enables them to meet challenges they're presented with and remain centered.

One of the areas in which we can help children to develop resilience is through the food that they eat. Each food has its own signature, or quality, depending on the conditions of growth and which part of the plant or animal is used as food. The signatures can be used to stimulate specific forces in the growing child and to balance one-sided tendencies. Food in its natural state, as close to nature as nature intended, is imbued with an etheric or life force that, when met by the individual through digestion, helps to build up our own life force. The life force is represented in a plant or animal by a mix of vitamins, minerals, enzymes and other compounds, and we respond to the mix of elements as a WHOLE. For example, the wheat berry contains in its sheath all the B vitamins, magnesium, manganese and fiber essential for digesting starch. Processed wheat flour has many, if not all, the vitamins and minerals leached out, leaving pure starch. The vitamins and minerals essential for digesting the starch are taken from body stores, leaving us depleted on other levels. Each step of food processing removes more of the life force. Vegetables that are peeled, chopped and stored in plastic bags in fridges with artificial lighting have already lost something.

One of the elements present in the signature of the food is warmth. In order to live comfortably in one's body, an optimal level of warmth is required; awareness of this is particularly important during winter. Some of us never feel warm enough and are constantly looking for the closest fire; others are overheated and need to get rid of excess warmth. As a rule, the color, fluid content and density of the food indicates the amount of warmth that the food will imbue to the body. Green foods tend to be cooling while yellow, orange and red foods tend to be warming. Watery foods will be more cooling than dense foods. The method of cooking may also be used to enhance temperature effects. Long, slow cooking imbues more warmth than short, fast cooking, and raw food is the most cooling.

Fats and oils are an essential part of the daily diet and stimulate the body to produce its own warmth. A reaction to the high prevalence of heart disease has caused many misunderstandings about fats. As well as stimulating warmth, fats and oils in the right balance modulate the immune system and provide protection for the nervous system. The fats, solid at room temperature and originating mostly from land animals in the form of milk, butter, cheese, chicken and mutton or beef, have the effect of hardening in the body. They need to be balanced out with the oils, which are liquid at room temperature and are extracted from seeds, nuts, certain fruits and fish. Within the oils are found three main types of fatty acid, the much spoken about omega 3, 6, and 9, all of which are needed in the diet. The omega 3 oils are typically deficient in our western diets, and one needs to make a conscious effort to include them, the main sources being fish, flax seeds or oil, and walnuts.

These are just a few of the many considerations in choosing one's food. Unless one makes a conscious effort, the diet can become one-sided and limited. An interesting exercise is to count how many times a day or week we eat wheat. Considering that there are at least another seven grains, each with their own subtle qualities, how are we restricting ourselves by not including them? To help children develop resilience, for now and for the rest of their lives, one can start to build healthy eating habits whereby their bodies become accustomed to a broad range of natural, fresh foods. In time they may begin to notice the difference in their sense of wellbeing and seek out these foods of their own accord.

Why Waldorf Works
From a Neuroscientific Perspective

by Regalena Melrose, MD

Why Waldorf works has more to do with how contemporary scientific research has shown that the brain develops and functions than Rudolf Steiner ever might have known in his time. Sure, the educator and founder of Waldorf education theorized convincingly about how children learn best, but until MRIs and other sophisticated measures of the brain were developed, we had no way to prove or disprove any of Steiner's theories with the kind of precision and accuracy we can now. An overwhelming body of evidence from the last 20 years of neuroscientific inquiry supports Steiner's theories, including some of the most fundamental foci of Waldorf education.

Three foci thrill me the most, both as a parent of a Waldorf student and as an international speaker on the topic of learning, behavior, and the brain: holism, play, and nature. An emphasis on all three is consistent with how the brain learns best: when the whole brain is engaged at any given moment, when its foundational neural connections have been given ample time to develop, and when it is in an optimally aroused state.

Knowing how the brain develops is essential to understanding why these three foci are so important to the success of any educational program. Let us learn first some basic fundamentals of the brain. First of all, it is "triune," that is, it has three parts. More importantly, not all three parts are fully developed at birth as we once believed. In fact, very little of a newborn's brain is "online" and "ready to go." When the brains of newborn babies are observed with MRI, we see that the only part of the brain that is lit up or active is the most primal part—the brain stem, sensing brain, or "animal brain," as it is also called. (Small underdeveloped parts of the auditory and visual cortices are the only exceptions.) This primal part of the brain is responsible for our experiences of arousal and stress. It kicks into high gear and mediates our "fight or flight" response when needed. I like to call it the "sensory brain" because it speaks only the language of sensations, the language that most consistently enables our survival. When we encounter a bear in the woods, for example, our words will not save us, but our heightened senses will.

The second and third parts of our brain—the limbic or feeling brain and the neocortex or thinking brain, respectively—begin to develop only after birth. This is critical new knowledge that provides a compelling answer to the long, highly debated question of "nature versus nurture." We now know that because we have use of only a very small part of our brain at birth, the brain is literally sculpted by the experiences we have interacting with others in the environment. It is not until 3 to 4 months of age, when the feeling brain has become activated by experience, that newborns are able to express more than just states of distress or contentment, as it does with only the sensory brain. At this somewhat older age, babies can share a wide range of emotions, thereby giving us a more social baby.

The third part of the brain, the neocortex, thinking brain, begins to develop after the limbic, feeling brain. Indications of this maturation include babbling between 6 and 9 months, a first word around the age of 1 year, and 2 to 3 words strung together by the age of 2 years. Whereas sensations are the language of the sensory brain and feelings are the language of the limbic brain, the neocortex speaks the language of words and mediates all of what most educators value. For example, the neocortex mediates impulse control and the abilities to plan ahead, to organize, and to understand that a choice we make now may continue to have consequences later. Empathy for another is mediated by the neocortex, as are our abilities to use ration, reason, and logic. We think and analyze with our neocortex and, of course, understand and have use of both receptive and expressive verbal language. If you've heard about "right brain" versus "left brain" functioning, it will make sense to you now that it is the neocortex that controls the functions of the left hemisphere whereas the sensing and feeling parts of the brain control the functions of the right hemisphere. The brain operates optimally when all its parts are equally developed, valued, and engaged. Why Waldorf works is because it does just that.

Steiner's approach to education is a holistic one. He recognized that our senses, feelings, and cognitions must all be actively engaged at each stage of development in order for students to maintain, over the long term, a joy and love of learning. Waldorf educators do not make the same mistake made by a number of other more traditional, conventional, and mainstream models of education. Waldorf educators do not overvalue the development of the neocortex and left brain to the exclusion of the right brain, that which senses and feels deeply. It does not focus at too young an age, before the brain is ready, on purely academic endeavors that attempt with rigor to engage a part of the brain that the child has little access to, the underdeveloped neocortex. (The neocortex is not fully developed until we are in our mid- to late 20s!) Instead, what Waldorf educators do successfully is involve and nourish the sensing, feeling parts of the brain, those easily accessed by young children, so that essential foundational neural connections needed for later academic learning are solidly laid.

Let me expand: You now know that the brain develops in a hierarchical fashion from more to less primitive, from the animal to the more uniquely human. What that means is that the healthy development of the more sophisticated neocortex *depends* upon the healthy development of the feeling, limbic brain, which *depends* upon the healthy development of the sensory brain. The problem with today's mainstream educational models is that they want the brain to walk before it can crawl. Well, let's be accurate: Most school systems today want children to *run* before they can crawl. We encounter proud parents who say, "My child was walking at 9 months! She didn't even need to crawl, just up and went! Isn't that terrific?" And what I want to say is, "No! No, that's not terrific! Push her to the floor! Make her crawl!" That might be an overzealous reaction, but it is grounded in sound knowledge that every single stage of development is essential to the next, laying a neural foundation to support what is to come. Our children need ample time and practice to "marinate in their mastery" of one skill or another, at each and every juncture of their development. This is not happening in enough schools across the country today, but it is happening at Waldorf schools.

Take the case of play. From the very beginning of a child's educational career at a Waldorf school, he or she is supported to play in a variety of different fashions and settings throughout the entire school day. Steiner knew that play is the invaluable foundation for any kind of healthy, human growth, including academic progress. And let's be clear about what kind of play this is. It is what Dr. David Elkind calls "the purest form of play: the unstructured, [spontaneous], self-motivated, imaginative, independent kind, where children initiate their own games and even invent their own rules." This kind of play, he warns us, is disappearing from our homes, schools, and neighborhoods at an alarming rate with great cost to the health, well-being, and achievement of our children.

Numerous studies have shown that play at every stage of development improves IQ, social-emotional functioning, learning, and academic performance. The findings of several studies conducted over a 4-year period found that spending one-third of the school day in physical education, art, and music improved not only physical fitness, but attitudes toward learning and test scores, according to Dr. Elkind. Furthermore, when the performance of children who attend academic preschools was compared to the performance of children who attend play-oriented preschools, the results showed no advantage in reading and math achievement for the "academic children," but did show that they had higher levels of test anxiety, were less creative, and had more negative attitudes toward school than did the "play children."

This is precisely the point we are missing in today's achievement-driven culture. We have bought into a myth in education that "more equals more." A formula of more time spent on academics, starting earlier in development, with more homework, is not increasing the output of our children. It's decreasing it! Cutting time out for the arts, physical activity, and time in nature so our children can spend more time reading, writing, and doing arithmetic is not the answer. It is the culprit. Our children are burning out and dropping out at catastrophic rates not just because more doesn't equal more, but also because it equals shut-down.

The brain functions its best only when in an optimum state of arousal. Our children cannot attend, listen, process information, retain, or perform well when in either an under- or an over-aroused state. Overwhelm is what causes these states. When, before the brain is ready, children are exposed to and required to participate in academics, media, technology, and organized play, such as team sports, the premature and often prolonged stress they experience can eventually shut the system down. Teachers all over the United States and Canada tell me they see "it" by the beginning of third grade. In far too many of their students, "the light has gone out." The joy, curiosity, and wonder that are essential to the learning process are already dulled by too much of one thing and not another.

Whereas the mainstream educational system today focuses almost exclusively on academics, a mostly left-brain function, Waldorf educators focus more on the whole brain, emphasizing the right hemisphere at each stage of development. Steiner could only have observed and therefore hypothesized that this keeps our children in the optimum zone of arousal where all of learning and adaptive behavior are possible. With current scientific findings, we now know he was right. Tapping into the sensory gifts of the right hemisphere provides the "flow" necessary for the marathon of achievement, not just the sprint.

Now that we've learned about the importance of holism and play to the learning process, let us consider the invaluable role of nature. A given within education is the engagement of the left brain. Learning almost always involves a verbal, analytical process. What is not a given, is the stimulation and expression of the right brain. The functions of the right hemisphere of the brain have somehow been deemed less important to the achievement and ultimate success of our children, at least "success" as most define it in the U.S. Our bodies are supported to move less, our minds to race more. Cuts have been made not only to recess and physical education, but also to creative endeavors such as theater, music and fine art, all of which make important contributions to the optimal functioning of the brain, achievement *and* success no matter how you define it. What does nature have to do with it? A whole lot, according to neuroscience: Nothing stimulates and resonates with the right brain more powerfully and, therefore, nothing keeps us in the optimum zone of arousal better than nature.

Remember, the optimum zone of arousal, when anxiety is neither too high nor too low, is the only physiological state within which all of learning and adaptive behavior is possible. Nature beautifully promotes that state. According to years of research recently compiled by Dr. Eeva Karjalainen, natural green settings reduce stress, improve mood, reduce anger and aggression, increase overall happiness, and even strengthen our immune system. Nature is one critical antidote to the increases in stress, overwhelm, burnout, and dropout we are witnessing in the educational system today. Lack of exposure to nature causes such a detrimental state to the brain, and is so pervasive today, that we have a name for it: "Nature Deficit Disorder." Dr. Karjalainen reports that "after stressful or concentration-demanding situations," we do not recover nearly as well in urban settings as we do in natural ones. When we experience nature, our blood pressure, heart rate, muscle tension, and level of stress hormones all decrease faster than when we are in urban settings. In children in particular, we know that ADHD symptoms are reduced when they are given the opportunity to play in green settings.

As a mother myself, I can't imagine a parent on earth that doesn't want all of these benefits and more for their children. I can't imagine that once parents and educators know the research findings pointing the way to optimal brain functioning, that any of us would ever agree to the kind of educational system we have now. The alternative of Waldorf exists, and I am grateful. I urge every parent to learn more about it and strongly consider it for their children. I am also aware, however, that not every parent has access to a Waldorf school for financial, geographical, or other reasons. For those parents and all of us really, I have an additional urging—that we vote, petition, write letters, make calls, and fight however we can to ensure that the reform about to take place in the current educational system be founded on the invaluable neuroscientific findings of the last 20 years. We must demand changes that are backed by sound science, based on how we know the brain works best, not just in the short-term, but for all the years to come.

About the Author: Dr. Regalena Melrose is a licensed clinical and credentialed school psychologist with nearly 20 years' experience working with children and adolescents in schools, clinical settings, and private practice. She is the author of several books including *You Can Heal Your Child: A Guide for Parents of Misdiagnosed, Stressed, Traumatized, and Otherwise Misunderstood Children* and the groundbreaking *Why Students Underachieve: What Educators and Parents Can Do about It*. Dr. Melrose is an international speaker on the effects of stress and trauma on the brain, learning, and behavior, and she maintains a private practice healing the effects of stress and trauma in children, adolescents, and adults in Long Beach, CA.

Note: Please visit www.whywaldorfworks.com; www.racetonowhere.com; www.americasangel.org; www.drmelrose.com; and www.waitingforsuperman.com for more information and resources.

The Senses

by Eileen M. Hutchins

We live as strangers in a world of light and color and sound. We behold around us many movements and forms, and yet we feel ourselves separate from them. And though within our own organism we have a realm which is more intimately ours, this too is a secret. For who can tell of the subtle changes which take place when he moves a hand or takes a step? Yet this inner world and the world around are made manifest to us through our senses, and if we would read their secrets, we need first to observe clearly that which is given. This is just where most of us fail, for we take so much for granted and we accept so much from the reports of others that we do not open our eyes and ears to that which is waiting to be revealed.

If we are willing to carefully consider the ways in which we can contact the world, we will find that our senses of perception are many more than the accepted five. Of the senses of smell, taste, color and sound we are well aware, even if we do not develop them very highly, for by means of them we connect ourselves with the world around, and their activity is accompanied by pleasure or pain. But let us consider for a moment how we are able to perceive our own organism. Many people, when questioned, reply, "We have a sense of feeling," but if the questioning is continued, the confusion becomes apparent, for feeling accompanies to a lesser or greater degree the functioning of all perceiving, and there is no special "feeling" sense. Yet in casual conversation we often speak more truly than we are aware. It is common to say, "I feel well" or "I feel ill," or after a good meal, "I have a sense of well-being." For we have a sense of our own condition, and this comes to a consciousness mostly when we are out of order or when, after illness, hunger or discomfort, we feel a renewing stream of life.

There is another way in which we are conscious of our life processes. When we are excited we feel our heart beat and our pulse throb, we feel stifled or our breath comes quickly. We are sensing the movement within our organism, and through this experience we are able also to relate ourselves to the movement of objects around us. But as we adjust ourselves in movement, another sense becomes active: We need to retain our balance. We are most aware of this sense when we are dizzy, or when a great effort is needed to keep our position, as in the beginnings of skating or in difficult mountaineering. We are not conscious, however, of the wonderful power by which we keep our upright position and with every step overcome the force of gravity. We see that in the case of these senses connected with our life processes we are very dimly aware of their functioning and only become awake to their activity when they are disturbed.

If we were to group our senses together in a certain connected series, we could so far arrange them as follows:
- Senses directed to our own organism:
  The senses of life or well-being, movement and balance
- Senses directed to the outer world:
  The senses of smell, taste, sight and hearing

But it is necessary to consider for a moment the sense of touch, and this sense should perhaps be the very first of our series, for without it we could not experience ourselves in our surroundings at all. In a way it is the lowest and yet the highest sense, for the first dim feeling of the most primitive animals is a kind of touch, a sensing of their surroundings, while one of the noblest strivings of man is to be 'in touch' with his fellow men.

If we now pass on to consider the senses directed to the outer world, we realize that those of "smell" and "taste" serve more to give pleasure to the physical body, while sight and hearing serve much more as the foundation for thought. There is another sense which is often overlooked and which is in a certain way connected with that of sight. Whereas our sense of sight gives us the perception of light manifesting itself in color, we have also a sense by which we detect warmth; and it is not difficult to see that this is quite distinct from the touch sense.

We may now add to our series as follows:
- Senses directed chiefly to our own organism:
  The senses of life or well-being, movement, balance and touch
- Senses directed chiefly to the outer world:
  The senses of smell, taste, sight, hearing and warmth

At the beginning of this article we came to the realization that there are more senses than the commonly acknowledged five. We recognized a certain group of senses chiefly directed to our own organism, and another group which relates us to the world around. I would now like to pass over to certain other senses which are little acknowledged as they are directed to a world which is no longer physically manifest, namely to the world of thought. In considering the senses directed to the outer world, we recognized that the senses of taste and smell are more experienced as giving physical pleasure, whereas those of sight and hearing give a basis for thinking.

Now we may take a step still further. For the average person a much stronger thought activity is needed to distinguish sound than to coordinate objects which appear before the eyes. If sounds are to take on a significance beyond the qualities of being loud or soft, harsh or melodious, thinking must become active. But together with this thinking moves also a further development of the perception. We perceive that sounds form a melody, or that words are spoken. Before we have weighed the meaning of the words, we perceive their utterance. Still further, we perceive whether the words express thought. Before we judge the thought to accept or reject it, we perceive that a thought is, as it were, offered for our consideration.

More than this, instead of observing objects in the outer world, we can perceive memories or thought images which we ourselves choose to contemplate. It is not for nothing that we use such phrases as "in my mind's eye." This inner perception is just as much an observing as is the case with external objects. We may, therefore, say that our sense of hearing leads over to a sense of speech and then to a sense of thought.

And now it is important to ask ourselves the question: "How do we perceive another human being?" We can, of course, see, touch and hear the person with whom we are present. But is this the highest extent of our perceiving? One hears of gypsies or hunters who can tell when another person is near even though they can see or hear nothing, for they sense the other person's presence. This type of sensing is not in the possession of the normal human being of today, but all who have had the experience of meeting someone and of feeling at once intimately connected know very well that we have a sense for perceiving the other human being which is more intimate than that of sight or sound.

To express this a little more clearly, here's an example. Perhaps we enter a room where there is a group of people, and we experience what is called a tense atmosphere, or perhaps on the other hand there is a friendly mood. No one, I think, will deny that this can be very vividly experienced, but on what does such an experience depend? It depends on the observing of very subtle relationships of human being with human being. It is possible to observe that when one human being enters a room immediately a restlessness is brought; another person may enter very quietly and there is a feeling of peace and tranquility. Our perceptions of such relationships are very little developed, and for the most part we do not try to cultivate that fine sensing of the personality of the other human being.

We might now in our series of the senses, arrange them as follows:
- Senses directed to our own organism:
  The senses of life or well-being, movement, balance and touch
- Senses directed to the outer world:
  The senses of smell, taste, sight, hearing and warmth
- Senses directed to the life of thought:
  Senses of hearing, speech, thought, of the other personality

And now I would like to make the arrangement in the following way:

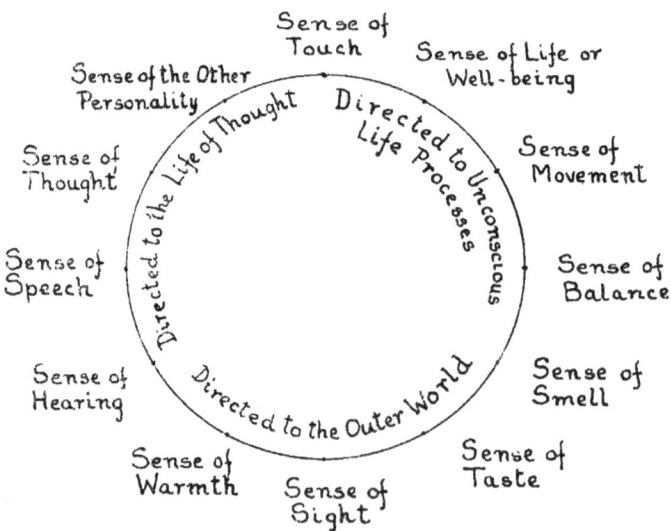

For here we may see how those senses connected with the bodily processes pass over to those directed to the outer world, and how these gradually become freer of the physical organism and lead to those directed to the thought life. And here once more we return to our sense of touch, but on a higher level. It is natural that we should speak of the instinctive feeling for what is pleasing to our fellow human beings as "tact," for it is a kind of touch in a higher realm. If we develop those senses which belong more to our thinking life, tact may become conscious, and we may be truly in touch with that which is most noble in the human being, his ideal life.

The senses may be pictured as a magic circle, a crown of twelve jewels, in the light of which the secrets of the world may be revealed. We have been given all that is needed to solve the mysteries of life, but the activity and the struggle are ours.

Note: This article came from Great Britain and was made into a pamphlet in 1975 by good friends Nathan and Yolanda McIniker who ran St. George Imprints. The clarity and value of the contents suggest that it come to the attention of contemporary readers.

The Training of Observation

by Eileen M. Hutchins

Most of those who have to do with education today come rather sadly to the conclusion that children are becoming more and more limited in their powers of observation. Within a certain field they are keenly awake, but they are blind and deaf to much that used to delight most of us when we were young. One can be put to shame by a child of six or seven when there is a question of the make of cars or of airplanes, but the average child of today has no interest for trees, flowers or birds and passes by the many aspects of nature with unseeing eyes.

Yet if we are willing to examine ourselves carefully, we will find that our own observation is but too often at fault. We are generally attentive only to that which has some practical use for us. We can be correct enough in taking in the main landmarks along a road that we need to travel, or in making a mental note of the appearance of someone whom it is important for us to recognize again. But is this observing? Is it not rather a collecting of characteristics? A true observing needs to be a living process.

If we watch a very young child, we see that he experiences the world around in a much more alive way than those who are older. Whether he is enchanted by the dancing of the sunlight on the wall or whether he is busy with the taking in of his food, he is entirely absorbed in his sense experiences. We may say he observes with his whole being. Or if we consider an older child of, say, eight or nine years, who has not been too much spoiled by a town life, we see that new experiences can often grip him with great intensity; that the meeting with new people can impress him so that a very strong liking or disliking is felt; and we are often astonished at the vividness with which children can recall certain details which were to us unimportant, and how these can be associated with great delight or horror. For the sense perceptions of the child of this age are very much bound up with his whole feeling life.

The grown-up has necessarily freed his power of observing from the intimate connection either with his organism, as is the case with the very young child, or with his sympathies and antipathies, as is the case with the child over seven; but only too often he has lost something of his connection with life as well. In our attempt to be objective and impersonal, we have dissociated ourselves from the world around. Observation has become an annotating process; it has ceased to be a living experience.

It is generally recognized in schools that observation should be trained. But it is our own powers which first need rekindling if we are to awaken those of the children. It is of little help if we teach them to collect specimens and make notes of various characteristics of stone, plant and animal, if we ourselves cannot experience the powers of nature and life by which these are surrounded. But such powers cannot be understood through an abstract intellectual thinking. We need to develop a certain attitude. If, for instance, we watch the sky day after day, the realization dawns: "Mighty powers are manifesting themselves, forever changing in cloud and light, in shadow and color." If at night we follow the solemn procession of the countless stars, then we feel within ourselves: "Here is expressed a wonderful harmony. If we follow these movements with devoted love, then more and more their nature is revealed."

Here our observing is an entering with our innermost being into that which is observed. We are not swayed by our sympathies or antipathies or by the influence of our organism; we selflessly make ourselves at one with what is around. We enter into the dynamic of the movements of nature, of the transforming life of the plants, of the sensations of the animal world, and of the riddles of human personalities. Here we cannot measure, weigh and count, for there is a point at which every measurement fails. It is not by means of the thermometer that we know the many qualities of warmth—from its powers of softening and dissolving to those of purifying and destroying, from its manifestations in human anger and indignation to those of generosity or love. These can be known only through an observing which is a being at one with the whole warmth activity.

Children by nature are able to enter these experiences, though more in a dream-like way. It is the life around which soon hardens them. It is important that as teachers and parents we strive to re-awaken such faculties within ourselves that theirs may also be rekindled.

The senses were once regarded as the twelve gateways to knowledge; but today many of these gateways remain closed. We do not wish to make the effort to seek for knowledge but would like to have it ready-made, given to us by others. Of how these ways may lead once more to an active thinking, it is necessary to speak another time.

Note: This article came from Great Britain and was made into a pamphlet in 1975 by good friends Nathan and Yolanda McIniker who ran St. George Imprints. The clarity and value of the contents suggest that it come to the attention of contemporary readers.

Observation and Thinking

by Eileen M. Hutchins

In the previous article on the "Senses," I drew attention to the fact that we have many more organs of perception than the usually acknowledged five. We are able on the one hand to perceive in a rather dim way the life processes in our own organism, and on the other to connect ourselves with the outside world, while beyond this we can develop perceptions which are connected with the world of thought. Yet however well we develop these senses, we are sooner or later led to a fundamental problem: "Do our senses really tell us the truth?" or "Are we able, by means of them, to grasp reality?"

We find many different viewpoints. On the one hand the average Westerner accepts the world as he knows it through his senses. He bases his life on the assumption that the objects around him are real and that thoughts and memories are shadowy reflections of the world of actual fact which is external to him. He feels that he approaches to truth when he widens his collection of data from the sense world. The Easterner, on the other hand, experiences the world around him as one of illusion, and he feels himself in touch with reality by escaping into the realm of his meditations.

How shall we harmonize these opposing views? Is one right and the other wrong, or have both something of the truth? Now we do not need to think very far to realize that the object world is not so reliable as we would believe it. It is only because we are so unobservant that we have come to regard it as in any way permanent. We are, in general, very much apt to take our surroundings for granted. If every day we pass through the same scene, then we feel a confidence that it remains there, unchanged in its essentials, from day to day. But supposing that we perform the following observation exercise.

Suppose that each morning, from the same window, we observe the landscape, carefully noting the salient features, and each morning before making this study we recall to memory as vividly as possible the view of the preceding day. Now, if on the first occasion we have observed with great care and concentration, we may perhaps feel satisfied that we really know it. Yet however strongly we are able to recall the image of yesterday, the new one will appear as astonishingly different. We may often, in fact, receive a certain shock.

Owing to the changing of light and shadow, of mist or wind, objects advance or retreat, group themselves differently or take on an entirely new character. A tree which one morning seems the center figure of the whole scene, on the following morning may well have retired into obscurity, while a more distant group stands forth in clear outline. One day with light frost and in clear air, the coloring may vary from turquoise blue to silver white, but the next, under lowering clouds, the tones pass over to shades of dark olive, indigo and purple. The far hills, which yesterday frowned darkly down upon the valley, today are as dim as the clouds above.

Whereas at first we tend to pay more attention to the actual objects, for instance, the shape and form of trees and buildings, we soon realize that these are not the most important elements. A flight of birds, the galloping of a horse and the strange wayward movements of the wind change the character of the scene. Still more we observe how the whole appearance is dependent on the quality of the light and, how under its spell, the objects appear and vanish, advance and retreat, grouping themselves, as it were, in the movements of some solemn dance.

The contrast each day between the memory picture and the new appearance can be very disquieting, for we soon come to this experience: It is impossible to grasp the scene at all, it is for ever escaping us, it is for ever new. It is disquieting, for we can rely on nothing. On the other hand, it is life-giving, for in the very quickening of our observation, we begin to feel ourselves living within the landscape and we receive strength and joy from its activity. We begin to realize with quickened feeling the forever-transforming power of the light.

By way of illustration, I have chosen an observation exercise connected with the sense of hearing. But it is possible to make similar exercises with the other senses. Suppose, for instance, we are accustomed to hearing every morning a certain sound, perhaps the ringing of a bell. We normally take it for granted that each morning it sounds just the same. But supposing we, first of all, recall the memory of the day before, and then listen to the sound. It will arise as a new experience. Though our memory may have been very accurate with regard to the pitch and strength of the note, yet it will seem, in a certain way, new. We may hear this bell a hundred times, but so long as we remain mere observers, we are bound to feel: "I still do not grasp that sound. I hear it again and again, and always if I pay true attention it has something of a new quality, but I do not really know it, its reality escapes me." For we come to a twofold realization that whatever we observe in a living way comes to us as a new experience, but that so long as we are mere observers, we cannot feel any certainty with regard to what we perceive.

The more we develop our observation, the more we realize this uncertainty. Our senses bring to us beautiful images, reflections of activities which take place around or within us. But so long as we are only observers, we cannot grasp the reality of these picture images. In order to read their meaning, we need to develop the activity of thinking.

We cannot come to any certain knowledge by means of our senses alone. We receive reflections or images of activities around us, but these images are repeatedly changing, and, as long as we remain mere observers, we cannot know the realities which express themselves in these changing pictures. We will now take a further step.

As soon as our thinking becomes active, we make connections between our many sense impressions; we discover in them certain rhythms and sequences. For example, suppose that we look at a plant. We have seen it in many different forms: in the dried, hard seed, in its gradual swelling and softening, in the sending down of the first rootlet, and in the uprearing and spreading out of the early leaves. We have marked its refinement into the blossom with its scent and honey, and with its pollen-bearing stamens; and we have noticed the gradual withdrawing of life from petal and leaf, and the concentrating of strength once more into the seed. Our many observations do not seem to us entirely scattered and isolated; we feel that we can bring them into some kind of harmony and gain a conception of a cycle in accordance with which the plant unfolds and withdraws again.

With many others of our sense impressions, we are able to form sequences. We observe rain falling from the clouds, so that streams become swollen and waterfalls tumultuous. We see once more mist and vapor rising from the seas and lakes and resting as clouds on the mountainside. Our sense impressions are on no occasion the same. Their variety is infinite. But nevertheless, we form from them the conception of a rhythm of activity.

But now it is important to ask ourselves the following question: "Through what power do we bring together our many separate impressions to form a sequence?" In a discussion on this question the answer was once given: "We piece together our different observations like a jigsaw puzzle, and then we have a picture of the whole." I think that anyone who has been in the habit of observing the world of nature would be unwilling to accept this answer. Nevertheless, it is not so easy to recognize at once how our thinking is able to perform this act.

We need to realize that all the forms which we see in nature are only external appearances which have been brought into being by invisible powers. The hoarfrost and the dew, the lightning and the will o' the wisp are the results of hidden activities. So long as we concentrate on observing the outer forms and then on patiently piecing these together, we shall certainly come to no understanding of the powers which bring these appearances to birth.

Let us approach with another attitude. Suppose we observe the plant in the following mood: "I have before me a seed: hard, dry and wrinkled. From my past experience I am aware that under the influence of warmth, of moisture and of light, this seed will expand and send roots down into the earth and leaves upward to the air, and blossoms will unfold toward the light. That which now is invisible within the seed will become visible. Yet it is possible also for me in the realm of my own thought to go through these same processes. I have the power to think through the many changing forms from seed to leaves to blossom and back once more in to the seed. That which is invisible can become visible to me within my life of thought."

The more we follow through such a process in relation to the actual observations we have made, the more it will have value for us. But I think all who have performed this exercise will realize that thinking is by no means a mere linking together of many images, but rather it is an activity which can be at one with the activities weaving behind the world of the sense perceptions.

We may perhaps ask ourselves of what importance it is that we can add from our own thinking a counterpart to what we observe. We may see the plant at any one stage of its existence, but we cannot say, "This is the true plant." For we know well that tomorrow it will be different. Yet in our thinking we can relate the one from which we see today to the cycle which we have experienced. Our sense observations are changing images, but with our thinking we grasp the reality of which the one impression is only, as it were, a mirage.

More than this, so long as we observe naïvely, many of our sense impressions do not seem to have any special connections together. But the more that thinking is active, the more we find that the apparently separate impressions are but single threads in a multitudinous interweaving. If I observe the plant at any stage of its unfolding, I find that if I wish to know it in its totality, I have no right to separate it from its surroundings. It is arbitrary to consider it apart from its whole setting in the light of sun, moon and stars, in the air, the moisture and the earth, and amid the accompanying life of bird, insect and beast. I am aware of all these through my power of observation, but only with my thinking can I find the manifold connections.

We cannot, therefore, say that the plant which we see before us is real and our thought about it only a reflection. For the plant, as I see it, is only one very small part of reality, and in my thinking I am able to connect it with the whole universe. My thinking is able to add to the sense impression that which is at present concealed from my sight. Without my power of observation I certainly could come to no knowledge, but if I remain imprisoned in my senses and regard the object world as the ultimate reality, I can experience only perpetual change and confusion.

One of the greatest difficulties in the way of our experiencing our thinking as an activity and a power is that we make no clear distinction between thinking and having thoughts. That person is considered to be a "thinking man" who has accumulated much knowledge. But thoughts are only the finished products of our thinking, and our whole outlook would be changed if we could find the courage to let go many of the thoughts which have now become dead shell and trust to the creative power of our thinking.

The world around us is changing fast, all that we have most valued is in danger, and we are likely to be witness to the downfall of a civilization. Yet he who is active in his thinking need not fear what life brings him. Our traditional judgments will prove inadequate, and the object world, if we rely upon it, will fail us. But our thinking has eternally the power to form life anew, for it is at one with the creative powers of the universe.

Note: This article came from Great Britain and was made into a pamphlet in 1975 by good friends Nathan and Yolanda McIniker who ran St. George Imprints. The clarity and value of the contents suggest that it come to the attention of contemporary readers.

The Rudolf Steiner College Bookstore has published a booklet with more of Eileen Hutchins' lectures, entitled *Observation, Thinking, the Senses*, available online at http://www.Item#1361, available at http://www.steinercollege.edu/store/product.php?productid=17806&cat=0&page=1.

The Activity of Thinking

by Eileen M. Hutchins

In my previous article on "Observation and Thinking," we came to the conclusion that in our thinking we can be at one with the creative powers of the world. This is easily said, however, and much more difficult to experience; for on all sides in life today, we find that this active thinking, of which we ourselves could be the conscious master, is very little recognized.

It is very difficult to expel the popular belief that to accumulate thoughts and be able to reproduce what others have taught is to be able to think. For this reason, we are cursed with a whole flood of books in which knowledge is made easy. Every branch of science, philosophy, literature and language is represented in editions wherein information is "potted" to suit the popular understanding. Even the Bible has been produced as a kind of novel. For we seek today to have the facts themselves rather than to develop the power by which we may find knowledge.

If we would know more of this mysterious power which is ours, then we need first to observe it. It is easy to observe our thoughts, but it is not so easy to observe and to think about our thinking. However, for a little while, let us make the attempt. If we consciously set ourselves a subject of thought and concentrate upon it for a short period, we can come to certain experiences. There are two different lines of thought which we might follow, and here people will certainly vary in regard to which they will find the more effective. We might, for example, concentrate upon an object for a few minutes and form around it all the thoughts which we are able to bring together. On the other hand, we might choose to hold for some while before our consciousness a picture image which has for us some content, perhaps an image of the rising sun.

Now I think all who have done even the simplest thinking exercises would agree that a complete concentration is by no means easy, and that our first experience is that our thoughts are all the while escaping us. Only with the greatest difficulty can we hold them in check. This attempt to master our thoughts can well be compared to the mastering of a spirited horse. Now, it may well be that many people consider that they have no difficulty in concentrating. For instance, the average person is doubtless able to carry through with the writing of a letter or the adding of his accounts without any undue wandering of the thoughts. But just in the exercises which we have set for ourselves and which are therefore free from the constraint of life's necessities, we experience the wayward nature of our thinking, and the effort to control it is a struggle.

If, however, we are willing to persevere in the struggle, and particularly if we are willing to do this repeatedly, we come to a further experience. We begin to feel within our thinking a certain life, and our thoughts, as it were, enter into existence. At first, while we are gathering around the chosen object all the thoughts which we are able to form, we may find that these are abstract. We are merely collecting together facts of information. But we can reach a higher level. For through our thinking we are able to discover the origin of the object we have chosen, whether it be from the realm of man's thoughts or from the life-powers of the universe. We are able to find the connections which underlie the many phenomena of nature, the invisible bonds which unite the objects of the world and our very selves within the universe. And at this stage our thinking ceases to be abstract. We experience, as it were, a draught from the well of life.

If we have chosen to contemplate a picture image, then, at first, this may appear before us with all its external characteristics, even, to a certain degree, photographically. But if, instead of concentrating on the outer form, we contemplate this picture with devotion and wonder, and try as far as possible to unite ourselves with the being and with the quality of that which we contemplate, then a new experience awakens. The picture becomes life-filled and vibrant. From this point our thinking is no longer only our own affair, our own individual activity. It seems now as though it streams forth as a light, enlivening and calling to life all upon which it shines.

It is not for nothing that in common speech we have such phrases as "to shed light upon a subject" or "to be an enlightened personality." For thinking was long ago experienced as a creative, light-giving activity, and it is only the modern world which conceives of it as a mechanical power which registers impressions and fits together the separate phenomena.

As we enter this world of thought and know it as something wider and greater than ourselves, we can perhaps begin to experience the birth of that tranquility which a true thinking can bring. We can perhaps now realize a little how the energy of our thoughts has something akin to the life processes of the plant. Each thought which we take, either from our own past judgments or from the researches of others, is as a seed—the condensed and contracted product of a powerful activity. But inasmuch as we brood and ponder over this thought, under the warmth of our enthusiasm it awakens to life, it strives to take on form as a living being, and it attains, at last, within our understanding, its light-filled true content, just as the plant bears its radiant flower—the inverted image of the heavenly world above. When thoughts are formulated and expressed, they become once more as seeds, to lie dormant until the activity is there which can awaken a true understanding.

It is of the greatest importance that we should experience once more the growth power and the light-radiating quality of our thinking, for only so can a new education arise. No new methods and theories can aid us at this moment when we are confronted with the downfall of a civilization. We need to develop the power to take that which the past has given, not as a tradition to be preserved in an abstract form, but as a seed from which can awaken new life. Many of our accredited facts will be disproved, and a great deal of our accumulated knowledge will be lost, for are we not at this moment witnessing the driving out or silencing of those who are bearers of learning? Man can only now find the strength to face life by developing powers of the spirit which can forever enable him to face life anew. He may pass through the darkness, for he has within him the power to create activity, life and light.

Certain experiences can be obtained by the training of our thinking, and this calls forth a question: "Of what value is this thought training for practical life?" It is natural that this question should be asked, for there are a great number of people who consider that to be practical in life, common sense is needed rather than thought and that the cultivation of one's thinking in the way suggested is a dangerous rather than a desirable schooling.

One is often met, for instance, with this type of argument: "What is said of the need to train our thinking is all very well, but first of all it is necessary to give man the right social conditions, and after that it will be possible to develop the spiritual life." Man first needs to be given his daily bread and only afterwards can God's will be done on earth as it is in Heaven.

Such an argument is the result of our modern world-outlook. For, consciously or unconsciously, most of us base our lives on the assumption that matter is the foundation from which the world has arisen and only gradually has life evolved. But if we think a little clearly from our own immediate observation and life-experience, such a theory is found to have no connection with realities.

We experience ourselves as surrounded by a world of objects. A number of these are created by man, while many others are there without his apparent cooperation, as the many forms which are bestowed by nature.

Now, if we first consider the objects which have been made by man, our argument can be very clearly demonstrated. We need only to ask ourselves: "Which came first, the object or the thought according to which the object was shaped?" and we realize that no man-made object would be there if man had not first planned it. For example, the plan and design of a house is destroyed; but so long as there are still human beings capable of conceiving plans, other houses will be built. Furthermore, if certain substances are lacking which the architect had first of all intended to use in his structure, he will certainly be able to find other materials to take their place. It becomes apparent that the thought is the origin, and according to the thought, matter is taken up and molded and formed.

It is perhaps more difficult to see the process in the case of the plants. Yet, if we observe the plant, we discover how it takes up the world of matter and transmutes it through the most wonderful and varied forms, gradually refining substance until it shines in the ethereal coloring of the flower and becomes more and more invisible in the pollen and scent. For anyone who truly observes, it is clear that these changes are due not to the chemical reactions of the substances, but to the life activity which can transform the material world; and this life-activity, while itself invisible, can withdraw for a while and again clothe itself in outer appearance in a perpetual rhythm. The substances which it takes up become infinitely complicated and are perpetually changing and transforming, but when they are laid aside again, they fall back once more into simpler forms and elements.

We can come to another experience. It is not our physical strength which determines our deeds; it is we who can be the controller of our strength. Our ability to perform and carry through what we have determined depends upon the guiding motive. In some cases, great love or fear impels human beings to deeds of which they are incapable according to the normal standard of their strength. Such feelings work with far greater power than our everyday consciousness. But it is possible to develop a consciousness which can transcend even such feelings, and deeds can be done which are held unbelievable from the judgment of only our physical capacities.

We can therefore come to the following conclusions:

- Thought controls matter;

- Life transforms substance;

- Spirit creates power.

And now we have to answer the statement: "Man needs bread before he can develop spirit." Let us for a moment consider it from the opposite point of view: "Bread will fail if man cannot discover spirit." Today, indeed, we give our children stones. For out of our materialistic outlook, we consider that the value of food depends on its chemical content. We imagine that substitute products from wood or coal, provided they contain the necessary chemical content, can be of equal food-value with the more natural products. For we reckon only with the reality of the world of substance and deny the world of life activity.

To one who has lived in the country, it is obvious that chemically purified bread has lost its life value. To understand the making of bread, we need to watch the wheat growing from green blade to golden ear. We need to realize how the flower is insignificant and withdrawn, so that all the forces of the plant may go to the forming of the grain, and how the starch which is usually contained within the root, is here formed within the ear where all the forces of the sun may enliven it. If we compare the flour of the wheat with that of the rye, the one so white and soft, the other greyer with its curious musty odor, we realize the sun-filled lightness of the wheat and the strong mineral salts of the rye. We then know that the powers and activities of these grains cannot be chemically analyzed or duplicated. The whole universe with its life processes takes part in their growth and we need these powers to nourish us. Chemical food may seem to satisfy, but we become hardened and gradually lose all power of creative thought.

We need to turn our attention once more to the world of life, not in a blind way as in some back-to-nature cult, but in the way of understanding and knowledge. If we are to work in harmony with the life-powers of the world, we need to know them, and knowledge can be obtained only through a systematic training of our observation and thinking.

If we imagine that we are practical when we consider only the world of objects as real, we are living in illusions, and it is just to dispel such illusions that the present crisis has come upon us. There has probably been no time in history when a greater number of people have lost all that they counted sure and certain. But such experiences can work for a new world outlook, for, in spite of the most materialistic world conceptions, one is driven by one's very fate to a recognition of the ephemeral nature of all matter and the eternal re-creative power of the spirit.

We cannot really act effectively in our daily lives without developing the activity of our thought, and that often the so-called common sense actions are those done out of routine and tradition. In continuation, I would like to show how the development of our thinking can enlighten the most commonplace duties and tasks of daily life.

Today, most people suffer the pain of having to do work which they cannot love. In almost every realm of life—in the office, the factory, the school and the home—much of the work is regarded as drudgery, and everyone longs for the free hours, the weekends and the holidays. According to our position and outlook on life, we regard our work either as a necessary routine by means of which we procure enough money to support ourselves and gain enjoyment or as the sorrow which man has to bear as his portion in earthly existence. Yet perhaps a little consideration may give us a deeper insight into our labor, so that through it we may find our connection with the world.

There was certainly a time when work was done with a very different impulse than it is today. Many of us can probably remember a grandmother or elderly relative who all her life had taken the greatest pride in the keeping of her home. She polished the stoves and the copper-pots, made all the bread and cake, to say nothing of the sausages and brawn. With the help of perhaps one sturdy family maid, she did the household cleaning and laundry and raised a large family of children. Even in her old age she rose early and worked late, and despised anyone who wished to escape from work in order to seek recreation.

Such characters can still be found in country places; but whereas half a century ago the average mother took such a pride in her home and family, it would be almost impossible today to find this type in any large village or town. What change has come in our life that the work which was once undertaken with pride is now regarded with distaste?

It is not generally recognized that our grandparents lived with quite another world outlook than that of today. The modern woman needs to go out into the world to find experience; she feels herself a prisoner if she stays at home. But our grandmothers, in the heart of their families, felt that they were in the midst of life. They still retained a feeling for the life-activity of the substances with which they dealt. They did not only look for labor saving devices, but were interested in the task for its own sake.

They had, for instance, something of a sense for the healthy nature of a wood-fire, and the blessing it bestows upon the bread baked among its ashes. They took joy in the beautiful shining copper of their pans or in the strong iron saucepans and the rounded form of the wooden spoons. They probably had very little learning, but they still felt something of the qualities of the metals and the materials with which they worked, and through these they felt themselves in connection with the substances of the universe.

Today, we are only anxious for our work to be done quickly and conveniently. We are delighted with aluminum pans and electric stoves, but it never occurs to us to consider that perhaps food cooked over wood or coal retains more of its life-giving power than that which has been heated by electricity, and that perhaps the iron and copper pans, which are certainly more difficult to work with, may nevertheless have a better influence on their contents than those of aluminum.

Our grandmothers still felt themselves at one with many life processes. They looked after the good friendly barn-door fowls, and perhaps shared in the making of the butter and the cheese. We are accustomed to buy all these from the shops like every other commodity and to think of them as merely so much food value.

Few consider today that the mood with which the work is done is of much importance; the main point is that the work is done efficiently. Yet in those days of big families and large gatherings, a great part of the joy in the work was gained from the fact that the kitchen was really the heart of the family life, and the meals were social gatherings. Anyone who has experienced, even if it is only from the tales of elders, the warmth and jollity of the big country family parties of long ago knows that the modern city socials with their intellectual diversions or unnatural dancing are poor affairs in comparison.

We have only to read a book like Schleich's *Those Were Good Days* (original title *Besonnte Vergangenheit*) to appreciate the joyous human enthusiasm which could live in the great family gatherings of seventy years ago. But in modern homes where the wife feels herself isolated in the flat, and hurries forth to serve on committees or attend meetings, and the husband comes back exhausted from the city, and where but too often an only child is delicate and difficult, there is little joy in human intercourse.

Yet though it is easy to praise the good old days, we certainly do not wish for their return. There was also a very dark side to the life of that time, and we can justly claim some progress. However, if we seriously face the facts, we have to acknowledge that, with all our advances, the enthusiasm for healthy hard work and the genuine warmhearted enthusiasm of the past are gone, and we cannot regain them in their old form. We can, however, find them in another way. Our grandparents still formed their lives out of their instinctive relationship with the world of nature and out of their practical experience; we have developed a more conscious thinking but have abstracted it from life so that our work has become so specialized that we can no longer find its world connection. We need to bring a living thinking to our labor and to find again our connection with the life of the universe. Wherever we stand, and whatever objects we deal with, we are able to reunite ourselves with world activities.

We can take a different interest in cooking if we recognize the egg, for example, as not only a necessary protein, but as a substance with its own individual place in the world of life. It is significant that the birds who of all creatures are the least bound by the law of gravity, nevertheless give over their young, before the time of their true birth, into the grasp of the earth. Yet the egg, which is so formless as far as the life of the young bird is concerned, mirrors within it the whole universe. We can see, as it were, an inverted universe in the golden round of the yolk floating in the clear liquid and surrounded by the alabaster shell. And just because the life powers have not yet started their work of forming the young organism, and the formless fluid is open to the influence of the whole world, the egg has its peculiar value for human food.

We can enliven our most distasteful tasks by the thinking which we bring to them. Washing-up is generally regarded as one of the most wearisome undertakings; yet we can find interest in our washing-up if, instead of wishing it finished so that we can escape to the cinema, we think a little of the objects which we wash and how they came into existence.

Suppose for a while we consider a cup. We are not concerned here with finding a dictionary definition, but with attempting to realize something of the origin of the object in the world of thought and the purpose which it serves. A cup, in order to be a drinking vessel, has both to receive and to give, for if it could only contain, it would be of little service. Its essential nature is service. Its essential nature is that it receives and holds only in order to give away again.

It is often held that man came to create cups through imitation; that first he drank from the cup of his hand, and then from a shell found perhaps by accident, and at last he came to model a form from clay in the likeness of these. But this is too superficial a view.

In all the world around we can experience the activities of receiving and giving. The mountain lake receives the water from the heavens and is forever giving it away to the streams and the rivers and back to the heavens once more. The human body at birth receives the life of soul and spirit and gives it away again at death; and it is no empty symbolism that represents the human body as a cup.

Man is surrounded in the world by the activities of receiving and giving, and although in past days he was not conscious of these in the way we are today, yet out of his living at one with these powers, he could form the objects in accordance with them.

From the humblest objects, whether given by nature or formed by man, we can, if we seek, find our way back again to the creative powers of the universe. There is no life so drab that it offers no point from which a view may be gained into the heavens. Though the old world is lost, out of conscious thinking we can again find ourselves at one with our work and with our fellow men.

Just as we cannot any longer live instinctively in harmony with natural powers, so we cannot now form a social life out of our blood relationships. There has to arise a new form of human intercourse and understanding, and of this it may be possible to speak further at another time.

Life today offers us a dark future, and we are often prone to fall into despair; for the estrangement of our Thinking from Life has not only brought barrenness in our inner life, but has also caused us to turn all our forces to destruction. Our ancestors also suffered; but they regarded their sufferings as the judgment of God for human wickedness, and their answer to it was a mood of repentance and devotion. Our suffering is the experience of desolation, and our answer to it has to be our striving to find again in every realm of life the working of the spirit and to unite ourselves once more with its power.

Through a living thinking, we are can bring interest even to the most distasteful of daily tasks and how, wherever we stand in the world, we can find once more our connection with the universe. In continuation I would like to reveal how, out of an active training of our thought, our human relationships also may become more enlightened.

Just as we can no longer work in the way of our grandparents, so our human connections can no longer depend on the bond of the blood. The family as the center of a social life no longer exists. It is notorious that nowadays relatives rarely have much sympathy for one another, and it is no longer a custom for children to follow their parents in the choice of a career. We are even very frequently faced with the picture of a family where the child seems a complete stranger to his parents. The build, the physiognomy and the temperament are so different that we are brought to wonder how such a child can appear in the particular family at all.

Not only has family life disintegrated, but there is no more the intimate relationship of colleague with colleague in the different professions and industries as there used to be, for instance, in the time of the guilds. We may work side by side in a factory, in an office or on the staff of a school, yet inwardly we are strangers, for our deepest experiences are not brought into our work at all. It frequently happens that workers who are intimately concerned in the same business are not even on speaking terms, and it is rare to find any creative social life arising from the common work together.

Yet the very fact that the life of family and of guild cannot any longer form the basis of human understanding causes us to turn our gaze in another direction. For we have come to the time when we have to form our human connections not out of blood relationships, nor out of the fact that we are employed in the same work, but out of the recognition of one another's true being.

This is by no means an easy task, for we are not really anxious in our acquaintance with people to probe beneath the surface. When we meet, we put up a cautious guard not to become too intimate at first in case afterwards we wish to withdraw. We prefer to talk only in superficialities or intellectual abstractions because to speak out of our most heartfelt human experiences would lead to an intimacy which we dare not face. In consequence, when we meet with someone, we recognize his temperament, his habits and customs and are aware of the sphere to which he belongs, but the one part of his being which is individual remains hidden. Yet all who look into their human relationships know that those connections which have really enriched their lives are not based merely on similarities of taste and habits or on a common sphere of life, but on the experience that their deepest beings have touched one another.

If we wish to train ourselves so that we can find a true basis of human understanding, then we need to develop our powers of observation so that we can penetrate further than the mere surface impressions. And for this we need a certain attitude of mind.

In all human intercourse there lie beneath the surface sympathies and antipathies. On the one hand these are not sufficiently recognized and on the other they are not understood. For if we feel an antipathy towards someone, we take good care to have as little to do with him as possible, while if we feel a warm sympathy and delight in another's company, we do not often enough consider: "Are we through our friendship developing something together? Are we bringing something to birth in the world?" It is important that we do not run away from our antipathies or only sun ourselves in our sympathies, but that with a certain objectivity we learn to understand out of what they arise. For it makes a great difference in our human connections if our antipathies arise because we see in the other personality our own failings, or because we belong to an entirely different stream of thought. In the former case, our antipathy is probably the greater. If we have ourselves suppressed certain faults, let us say perhaps that we have a certain hidden conceit, then the appearance of this failing in another gives us the greatest annoyance. Or, if we give way to our natural disposition and we are perhaps be of a melancholy temperament, then we are not likely to be pleased with another who resembles us in this. We are prone to think: "Why on earth should he be so melancholy, he has no reason for it."

It is otherwise if we belong to a different stream of thought. Perhaps at first we feel no antipathy at all; we may even be drawn to one another! But the difficulties arise as soon as we have to work together in any very intimate way. For we soon realize that our most earnest strivings meet with complete lack of understanding. However much we may charm one another on the surface, we cannot pass this barrier. Such a discovery can lead to great suffering between those who thought at first that they were very much at one.

In each case, it is possible to overcome antipathy through understanding. In the first place, if we try to make good our own failings, we can view those of others calmly, and perhaps even discover that fundamentally we have much in common and can work in a most positive way. Or in cases where a personality arouses antagonism through an unfortunate manner, we can perhaps surmount this difficulty through a quiet observation which reveals to us the cause. One who has had an unloved childhood may easily in later life be cold and sullen, but in his real being he may have quite other feelings. Our patience to bear with his outer mannerisms may lead us to find the hidden qualities. It is often the case that those who later have become our most valued colleagues had at first aroused our strongest antipathy, while many for whom we experienced abounding sympathy failed us in our time of need.

An entirely different approach is required to one who belongs to another stream of thought than ourselves. We may be in sympathy with his temperament, yet we need to develop the greatest understanding and tolerance for his point of view and leave him the freedom to act in his own way, provided he does not infringe upon our realm of responsibility. But it is a mistake to imagine that we can carry through any task together when we are inspired by entirely different impulses. A compromise with those who have a different aim can satisfy neither, and brings any creative work to a kind of standstill. It is, however, possible to seek again and again for a foundation where we are at one, for inasmuch as we are all human beings living in the same period of earth existence, some connection is necessarily there.

If with this objective attitude we learn to read behind the outer symptoms and to understand what underlies our sympathies and antipathies, we can begin to develop the ability to recognize our true connections with one another. Mostly we do not cultivate the special kind of awakeness necessary for this recognition. Occasionally we meet with a person of some position who has very great insight and in one interview can judge both those who will be of service to him and those who are completely unsuitable. But since the days of examinations, testimonials and approval by committee, this gift is less likely to be found. Yet certain people have it to a marked degree. I will give an illustration from life.

There lived a certain man of considerable ability and vigor, yet by no means a genius, and he worked in quite an ordinary sphere of life. One day, a girl whom he did not know came into his shop, and he immediately said to a friend, "Do you see that girl? She will be my wife." He thereupon took pains to discover her family and become introduced. He was soon a regular visitor, and in the course of time proposed to the girl. She refused him. However, he continued to visit and proposed again. She still refused. But he persevered and upon the third time of proposal she accepted him. They suited one another ideally and lived long and happily together.

In the biographies of men of genius we can find much more striking examples of this type of sudden intuition. For instance it happened to both Garibaldi and Schleich that the moment each saw the girl whom he was later to marry, he knew: "She is to be my wife." But I have given the above example to show that this faculty is not the special gift of genius but can be possessed by very ordinary people. I think nearly everyone will have had the experience one time in his life that in meeting some stranger, he spoke to him suddenly in the spur of the moment for no preconceived reason, and that from this developed a connection of the greatest importance in the lives of both.

Through such connections we learn of the power which hate and love can work in the world. In these days of so-called objective thinking, we accept the assumption that if one man does a piece of work in two days, two men will do it in one; and where we are concerned with purely mechanical labor, this formula will undoubtedly prove more or less correct. But if anyone has ever been responsible for creating out of his own initiative, he knows very well that it is fundamental for those who work with him to be in sympathy with his aims. And if he has the good fortune to find a friend of such a nature that the two can mutually inspire one another, then it certainly is not a case of two men doing the work in half the time, but of a union from which an entirely new creation arises.

On the other hand, the presence of a critic who stirs up doubt and suspicion can completely prevent a work from being accomplished at all. This is naturally recognized in obvious cases, but in ordinary life we do not sufficiently observe how opposition and criticism work with deadly certainty to destroy all that they touch, while hope and confidence can bring an undreamed of renewal of life. This is the secret of the magic of the Middle Ages: the black magic of hate and the white magic of love. For love and hate can indeed work in ways quite beyond our materialistic thinking, and unless we can develop an observation of these hidden streams which flow through all human intercourse, we fail to reckon with some of the most powerful forces in the world.

Today we are facing the onslaught of just such powerful forces. We can indeed meet destruction with destruction and hate with hate. But there is only one power which is greater than destruction and hate, and that is the love which is born of wisdom. Whether we can overcome our enemy with material weapons or not, there is only one way that freedom can be won for mankind, and that is through the spiritual strength which arises from a true knowledge of man.

Note: This article came from Great Britain and was made into a pamphlet in 1975 by good friends Nathan and Yolanda McIniker who ran St. George Imprints. The clarity and value of the contents suggest that it come to the attention of contemporary readers.

The Rudolf Steiner College Bookstore has published a booklet with more of Eileen Hutchins' lectures, entitled *Observation, Thinking, the Senses*, available online at http://www.Item#1361, available at http://www.steinercollege.edu/store/product.php?productid=17806&cat=0&page=1.

An Education for Our Time

by Christof Wiechert
translated by Margot M. Saar

In this article we investigate whether the first years at the Stuttgart Waldorf School can be seen as prototypical for the development of schools and teachers in general. It tries to establish whether we can benefit today from the events that took place in the six years between 1919 and 1925, while this first school was led by Rudolf Steiner. Can we find something archetypal in these events that could give direction to the development of teachers and schools in the 21st century?

Sources

In order to be able to answer these questions, we need to consult the relevant sources, especially the lectures Rudolf Steiner gave to the teachers of the first Waldorf school. What interactions do we find concealed there? Today's readers of Steiner's lectures are used to looking for general information such as knowledge of the human being. The majority of lectures on education was given to a general audience, with only a few of them addressing the same group of specialists, i.e., the college of teachers of the first Steiner Waldorf School in Stuttgart. (In Steiner's times this consisted of 12 colleagues; by the beginning of class 6 the number had risen to 49). The following lectures were given to this relatively small group of people:

> *Study of Man* (later published as *The Foundations of Human Experience*)
> *Practical Advice to Teachers, Discussions with Teachers* (Stuttgart, 21 August–6 September 1919; CW 293, 294, 295)
> *Balance in Teaching* (Stuttgart, 15–22 September 1920; CW 302a)
> *Waldorf Education for Adolescents* (*Supplementary Course*). (Stuttgart, 12–19 June 1921; CW 302)
> *Adolescence – Ripe for What?* (Stuttgart, 21–22 June 1922; CW 302a)

> *Art in the Light of Mystery Wisdom* (Two lectures, Stuttgart, 7 and 8 March 1923; CW 283)
> *Deeper Insights into Education: The Waldorf Approach* (Stuttgart, 15 and 16 October 1923; CW 302a)

There are two other important volumes:

> The 70 teachers' conferences with Rudolf Steiner: *Faculty Meetings with Rudolf Steiner* (CW 300 a-c)
> Rudolf Steiner in the *Waldorf School—Lectures and Addresses to Children, Parents and Teachers*. This includes addresses at monthly school festivals, seasonal festivals and parent evenings.

The lectures mentioned were given to one and the same audience. We will now try to investigate how the lectures responded to the evolving situation at the school.

Stage 1: *The Study of Man*

After the opening address on the eve of the Teachers' Seminar where Steiner outlined the school's administrative set-up in a few sentences ('not bureaucratically, but collegially … in a republican way. … Each one of us must be completely responsible. We can create a replacement for the supervision of the School Board as we form this preparatory course and, through the work, receive what unifies the school'[1]), the first lecture was presented on the following morning.

With simple words, the significance and depth of which can be grasped only gradually, a link is established between a new education and human evolution. A connection is created to the spiritual world and to entities whose deepest concern is the development of human beings. Reference is made to the 15th century as the starting point of the development, the consequences of which we experience today. The concentration of intelligence on purely worldly aspects, which was necessary for human freedom to unfold, gave rise not only to science and technology, but also to materialism and egoism. '… all of modern culture, right into the spiritual areas, is based upon human self-interest.' It is pointed out that the religions tend to focus on the after-life as the time when everyone's future lies while forgetting about the time before birth. It is the teacher's task to explore the life before birth: 'Our form of educating can have the correct attitude only when we are aware that our work with young people is a continuation of what higher beings have done before birth.'[2]

How can this be achieved in practice? Think of a child study. The first step is the forming of a picture of the pupil as he or she appears in space and time. In order to understand this picture we have to go a step further. How did the pupil come to develop in this way? It is easy to find out as long as one avoids the temptation of applying superficial psychology (which never leads to any insight or knowledge). We come to an understanding of the inner essence of a pupil if we ask how ether body and physical body, for instance, relate to one another, or how the soul (astral) works on the 'learning body' (ether body). How did spirit soul (or soul spirit) and life body find each other? What expresses itself in which way? We experience immediately, if we practice this way of asking questions, how we move in a realm of 'pure air' where we can sense the becoming and the essence of the human being. We begin to understand.

Those of you who attempt this, when meditating on a pupil for example, know from experience that it works only if you manage not to put yourself into the foreground. You have to be open, without preconception; the 'not I, but the pupil in me' approach will allow you to develop a sense for the pre-earthly intentions through observing the pupils. If I manage to take hold of these intentions as ideas, I will be able to fuse them into an ideal. Pedagogical inspiration becomes possible, acting in harmony with what wants to come to life. It arises out of the interest in the pre-earthly aspects that reveal themselves in the different parts of the human organization. (Steiner gave evidence of this capacity in the course of more than a hundred child studies.) It is easily forgotten that the understanding and anticipating of the pupils' temperaments is also a way of overcoming 'cultural egotism.' The temperament says something about how the life before birth weaves into the life after birth. When studying the pupils' temperaments the teacher has to hold his own temperament back and this allows him to build a bridge to the child, to the pupil. Then the child, the pupil, will come towards him.[3]

Let us turn to the end of *The Foundations of Human Experience* (*Study of Man*) and *Discussions with Teachers*. The last lecture deals with the surprising significance of the image, of speaking in images, of keeping the intellectual flexible. The importance of imagination is emphasized, especially on the threshold to adolescence (ages 12 to 15).⁴ The process culminated on September 6 with the presentation of the seven virtues of the teacher—the first three at the end of the last lecture of *The Foundations of Human Experience* (*Study of Man*) —'Imbue yourself with the power of imagination, have courage for the truth, sharpen your feeling for responsibility of soul,' the remaining four at the end of *Discussions with Teachers*: 'The teacher must be a man of initiative, a man of interest in the being of the whole world and of humanity, a man, who never makes a compromise in his heart and mind with what is untrue (especially in the way we present our subjects) and he must never get stale or grow sour.'

How does one deal with these virtues? The last four represent faculties of the temperaments; they are virtues that can be exercised in one's daily work. Initiative: Shall I make the phone call tonight or wait until tomorrow? Interest: These parents are foreign to me, can I still summon up an interest in them? This colleague gets on my nerves, but that is interesting! This student walks in such a strange way, as if the ground beneath him was hurting him. What does that indicate? Am I really interested in the lesson material that I have to present just now? Whether I have a strong or only a lukewarm interest in the subject matter affects the liveliness of my teaching. In the compromise: 'He must never compromise with untruth, for if he did so we should see how through many channels untruth would find its way into our teaching, especially in the way we present our subjects.'⁵

This is a direct reference to the teaching method and there are many channels open today through which untruth can creep into our teaching. Is it not much more practical to have an established method for teaching a foreign language? Should I not just use exercises from these excellent publications on basic maths, spelling, elementary physics? There are so many useful things. We could also call this the virtue of faithfulness. I am faithful to a method which I shape in the truest possible way while constantly renewing it to keep my teaching alive. Every adult has some melancholy which, depending on his overall temperament, struggles with staleness and sourness to a greater or lesser degree. From a certain age it is always lurking around the corner. Am I sufficiently aware of it? Observing each other's lessons is good prophylaxis. (Why do you work with the children in this way? Asking is appropriate, judging is not.) The first three virtues are of a different nature. They cannot be practiced in our day-to-day work. We all know it from experience: imagination, speaking in images, being inspired—this I cannot develop while standing in front of the class. If I have it, it is as a result of different processes. We are referring to ways of educating oneself. Acquiring knowledge of the human being in the three stages described by Steiner elsewhere is one path that leads to imagination, life and the 'profound power of ingenuity that you need when facing the child you are to educate.'[6]

Again and again, we are faced with the immensity of the opening words of *The Foundations of Human Experience* (*Study of Man*). They resound as from other worlds: 'My dear friends, we can accomplish our work only if we do not see it as simply a matter of intellect or feeling, but, in the highest sense, as a moral spiritual task. Therefore, you will understand why, as we begin this work today, we first reflect on the connection we wish to create from the very beginning between our activity and the spiritual worlds.'

We ask ourselves whether the 'moral spiritual' is not the realm referred to as truth and responsibility in the first three virtues? For all that is spiritual surely is responsibility, all that is moral surely is rooted in truth. We see a gleam of the future of humankind: goodness, beauty, truth as in Goethe's Fairy Tale or as in the Christ words 'I am the way, the truth and the life.' 'Imbue yourself with the power of imagination' can be seen as the way in education, because Steiner once described education as a 'form of normal life.'[7] After presenting the last four virtues in the closing words to the fifteenth discussion with teachers, Steiner added a more personal note: 'For me this Waldorf school will be a veritable child of concern.' He exhorted the teachers to work together and to live in awareness of 'the spiritual powers that guide the cosmos ….they will inspire our lives.' Shortly before the first Waldorf school opened he asked the teachers to promise him to keep this awareness alive.[8] The classrooms were not ready yet when the school opened with a festive celebration on September 7. Lessons could only begin on 16 September, by which time Steiner had left for Berlin. During the first school year, Steiner had fourteen meetings with the teachers, and three more took place at the end of July 1920 in preparation for the second school year. The first school year started with 12 teachers, 8 classes and 256 students which means that the average class had 32 pupils and there was 1 teacher for every 21 students (today the ratio is on average 1:10). The second year started with 19 teachers, 11 classes and 420 pupils which means the average class had 38 pupils and the teacher-pupil ratio was 1:22. These numbers alone justify the expression 'child of concern.'

Stage 2

Five days before the beginning of the second school year, Steiner gave four lectures to the teachers which were intended as a 'supplement' to the introductory lectures on education given in the previous year (*Study of Man*). The preparations for the second school year were so comprehensive, however, that he doubted whether he could manage more than 'scanty introductory words.' He wanted to speak about 'the teacher, the educator' and 'the nature of the esoteric.' The first lecture dealt with the 'condition of misery' in the education of the young which had arisen due to the fact that humankind 'in essential things really made itself dependent … on the kind of thinking and feeling peculiar to the West.' Fichte, Herder, Goethe were no longer understood. What Herder and Fichte wanted, an art of education, had been turned into the opposite. Steiner offered examples for this view and concluded the lecture with the words: 'But with regard to what has to be given for the art of education, we have something to give the world from Central Europe which no one else can give.'

It hardly needs pointing out that he is not referring to geographical or national aspects, but to spiritual streams. To whom was Steiner saying this? He was addressing the college of teachers of the first Waldorf school, which had just completed the first school year with eight classes and had grown to 19 colleagues. Was it necessary to refer these individuals to the way Western man thought and felt? Did they no longer understand German Idealism? Did they of all people need to be told in depth that their success as educators depended on how much they themselves learned from their teaching? This 'inward humility' which grows out of the insight 'that the art of education must proceed from life and that it cannot proceed from abstract scientific thought.' Herder, Fichte, Jean Paul, Schiller represented 'a life-infused education,' 'a way of educating drawn directly from life.' Steiner called this the 'Central European education impulse.' References to it will 'annoy' the scientific thinkers.[9] This was the situation after one year of Waldorf education. Reading this in 2009 we know: it is still (and again) the main motif in the art of education. Probably due to the experiences of the first school year, Steiner urgently pleaded for a 'new education appropriate to the time,' an art of education drawn from life itself.

Today the phrase 'art of education' is still ruffling feathers. What were the consequences? In the lectures mentioned Steiner did not return to the seven virtues of the teacher, but spoke of three fundamental forces in teaching. If we bear in mind that the quality of an organism is determined by the sum total of forces that its members are able to summon up, we realize what Steiner achieved with lectures 2 and 3 of *Balance in Teaching*.

He spoke to the teachers about reverence, enthusiasm and the protective gesture. Reverence for what the child brings with him from his life before birth, for what determines his existence. Enthusiasm for what the pupil can become in future with our help. Protectiveness to ensure that the pedagogic reality in the here and now remains appropriate to the child's age. These forces or attitudes, by the way, go with at least two, if not all three, gestures that years later came to represent the higher schooling path of the Michael School.

What else did Steiner give the teachers with these few lectures? Next to the pedagogical contents he conveyed to them two ways of transforming their teaching by filling it with life inspired by the Central European spirit. He showed them how to realize their 'power of ingenuity,' i.e., their pedagogical imagination and intuition. The first can be practiced with the help of inner pictures; Steiner called them meditative images in this context. Intuition is practiced by following the digestive process that takes place after one has absorbed spiritual scientific content. The 'vigorous power of ingenuity you need when facing the children you are educating' is kindled if one develops mental images of how visual and auditory perception relate to one another in a crossing over process; how the audible is perceived in the will (or memory) region of the visible; how the visible is remembered in the perception region of the audible; how these two principles of time and space in fact form the human body.

Such 'pictures' (or meditative images) can also be derived from the second lecture by considering the two streams: the sculptural and intellectual forces that come from the head or use it as transition and the musical forces that stream in from the outside world. The first work from the outside as attack and from the inside as defense. The latter where the attack comes as from inside are attenuated by music and speech instruction. Experience shows that such images, if they are again and again placed before the inner eye, strongly inspire the day-to-day work of the teacher.

The second important indication that Steiner gave to the teachers after their first year of teaching referred to the threefold approach to attaining knowledge of the human being: studying contents, coming to understand what has been studied through meditation (calling up images again and again), 'and finally we have a remembering of the knowledge of the human being out of the spirit. This means teaching creatively out of the spirit; the art of education comes about and takes form.'[10]

As the crowning we have the practical examples that illustrate how our teaching works on the relationship between the I and the body. What seemed like an abstract request the year before ('the task of education conceived in the spiritual sense is to bring the soul-spirit into harmony with the life body')[11] is now explained in detail: how this harmonizing of the upper and lower human being proceeds. How the I settles in the body without being 'caught' in it. It all depends on how elements of a sculptural, musical and intellectual nature and elements of memory and speech alternate within the lesson. The impact of the various subjects is also explained: whether they help the I to 'settle' or achieve the opposite. It is like the ultimate description of the artistic approach to teaching.

In summary we can say that Steiner obviously deemed it necessary in September 1920, after one year of Waldorf education, to confer with the teachers on the educational impulse that is drawn from life and not from science. The seven virtues of 1919 were extended by the three forces that relate to the pupils' past, present and future. On the basis of this he used higher considerations regarding the human being to point out two possible paths, one of which is more inspirative ('the vigorous power of ingenuity') and the other more intuitive ('teaching creatively out of the spirit').

At the end Steiner demonstrated the artistic approach to education and how it 'regulates' the relationship between the I and the body: the essential task of education. I would suggest that this was exactly what the teachers of the first Waldorf school needed after one year. It is what Steiner identified based on the experience of this first year.

We ask ourselves now: how is it with these qualities in 2011? Are they an inherent and identifying component of the Waldorf school? Are they cultivated in the right way in the teacher training seminars and in teachers' meetings? Have we understood that this education has to be drawn from life, from the living experience of teaching rather than from imposed parameters of whatever description? These four lectures alone support what is said throughout the school movement, that if Steiner had to do it all over again, he would drastically change course and steer towards the artistic. We need not worry about the authenticity of this statement. It is the essence of these lectures.

Stage 3

Another year later, eight days before the beginning of the third school year, Steiner gave eight lectures to the teachers (later published as *Waldorf Education for Adolescents*). Unlike those published in *Balance in Teaching*, these lectures do not explicitly tie in with *The Foundations of Human Experience (Study of Man)*. By the beginning of this school year the school had almost doubled in size: 540 pupils in 15 classes (36 per class). The teacher-student ratio was 1:18. Steiner never complained about the fast growth despite the fact that the financial problems were enormous. Can we assume that the lectures on the *Meditatively Acquired Knowledge of the Human Being* (cf. *Balance in Teaching*) had made an impact on the individual teachers? Steiner began by looking back over the first two years and concluded: 'In order to prevent a possible misunderstanding of what I am going to say today, I can assure you that I have noticed and appreciated the progress made during these two years. The way you are teaching—the presentation of subjects—is already such that it can be said: You have, in an extraordinarily healthy way, fused with the goals of these tasks.' It sounds like a report for the teachers. The eight lectures embrace the richest content, always in keeping with *Practical Advice to Teachers* and with frequent excursions to the study of the human being. The sense of urgency that prevailed in *Balance in Teaching* has abated. The connection of memory and feeling, the work with children who have poor or rich imagination, with cosmic and earthly children – the teaching methods are extended. This culminates in Lecture 3 in which the three essential steps of teaching are explained that happen over a period of two (not three!!) days so that 'the three parts of the threefold human being can interact, they are allowed to harmonize in the right way.' The lectures that deal with adolescence, with the diverging male and female constitution, return to *The Foundations of Human Experience (Study of Man)*. The lectures are not just intellectually pleasing; Steiner, with his subtle sense of humor, again proved himself an expert on the adolescent soul. The presentation moves on to explain at a deeper level the 'understanding of the world' that is needed for teaching adolescents. The teacher needs to become a representative of the world. Those teachers who have nothing narrow-minded about them, represent the 'wide world.' The students begin to choose their authorities and develop their first life ideals inspired by the authenticity of their teachers. Here lies also the secret of a fruitful living together of different generations. The lectures end with the suggestion that one should feel as if the spirit disperses itself among the college of teachers like a living cloud, as if living spirits were called on to help to instill spirituality in the souls: a 'prayer-like' rising up to the spirit. 'Life' or vibrancy is a recurring motif. The conclusion is a parenthesis to the first lecture of *The Foundations of Human Experience* (*Study of Man*) which deals with the spiritual task of education. It returns in the form of a meditation:

> We have the will to work, letting flow into our work, that which from out of the spiritual world, in soul and spirit, in life and body, strives to become human in us.

In *The Foundations of Human Experience* it was:

> The task of education conceived in the spiritual sense is to bring the soul-spirit into harmony with the life body.

What is the difference? The 'meditation' focuses on the teacher himself: 'strives to become human in us.' Education is self-education. In summary: *The Supplementary Course* is in character closer to *Practical Advice to Teachers*, due to the fact that a tenth class was to start next to class 9. Detailed curriculum indications were developed in the teachers' meetings. The lectures introduced three essentially new practical methods together with suggestions for their application: the cosmic and earthly orientation of the interest (the astral viewpoint), children with rich and poor imagination (which is more to do with the ability to remember, the etheric viewpoint) and the threefold approach to teaching (over two days) that applies to all lesson contents from the age when main lessons convey subject-matter as such. This is followed by an extended psychology of adolescence.[12] We can imagine that the teachers were delighted about these eight lectures. Not only was the review of the first two years extremely encouraging, the lectures also opened up an unclouded, widened horizon.

Stage 4

Steiner's meetings with the teachers have so far not been considered in this paper. When I turn to them now it is with the inner conviction that it is high time that this treasure of 70 teachers' meetings is published in scientific edition in order to throw light on the development of the art of education in practice. The teachers were not able to apply in practice the indications given in the *Supplementary Course*. At the end of the third school year the students of class 10 asked for a meeting with Rudolf Steiner. They complained about their teachers, about the 'lecturing' (we call it today 'chalk and talk,' frontal tuition with merely rhetorical questions), about the teachers' lack of interest, about 'not having learned anything.'

Steiner looked into the situation and, based on his findings, he arranged for a change of teachers for most of the main subjects, right at the beginning of the fourth school year for these students who were now class 11. 'We did not consider enough what I said at the beginning of the school year with regard to these children.'

The teachers, in their turn, accused the students of showing a lack of will in their independent work. Steiner answered: 'That is a problem that lies with the children, and that one we do not need to discuss. What is important now is how we cope with the children.'[13]

The situation continued, vehemently, into the following year. The students became morally neglected, got into trouble and some of them had to be asked to leave. Steiner could see no other way but to blame the state of affairs on the teachers: their lack of interest in the pupils, the absence of contact, the lecturing instead of teaching that had become the rule, the general sloppiness. Neither teachers nor students were fully engaged in the lessons. Social tensions made the situation worse when it was suggested that a small administrative circle should be established. Strong mutual distrust became apparent. The teachers' meetings as such were put into question. Steiner: 'I feel like I have contracted lockjaw from the bad attitude toward the meetings.'

Questions of discipline recurred because the teachers felt powerless. Steiner called on the foreign language teachers to work together and find a way of teaching the language instead of complaining to each other about the students' lack of understanding. The meeting of February 6, 1923, is recommended to all who wish to experience how dramatic a situation it was. (This is the meeting where Steiner spoke about large-headed and small-headed children; it is also the meeting where the failed grammar lesson is described and its effect on the threefoldness.)[14] In the third school year which had started so pleasantly only seven meetings with teachers took place. During the difficult fourth and fifth years Steiner made it possible to attend 15 meetings per year. In the autumn of 1923 a severe crisis loomed as teachers struggled under the pressure of the immense and partly new demands. Following a phone call Steiner managed to fit in a visit to the school. He spent October 15 and 16 in Stuttgart, giving three lectures and meeting with the teachers. The exhausted teaching staff heard lectures that belong to the most difficult of Steiner's presentations on education. As with the opening lecture in *Balance in Teaching*, the beginning was unexpected: Gymnast, rhetorician, professor have to undergo a metamorphosis. The weakness of the professor is described: 'Today we usually think because we do not know what else to do, and that is why we have so few real thoughts.'

The second and third lecture are given on October 16 with the teachers' meeting taking place in between.[15] What is the main theme of these presentations? As Steiner spoke about curative education for the first time on February 6, he explained the surprising difference between the healing processes in medicine and in education. They work at different levels. Totally new aspects arise with regard to the knowledge of the human being: 'There are the movements of walking, grasping, the movement of the limbs, outer changes of location, the activity in the process of nourishment, the rhythmic activity—which is through and through a healing activity—and the perceiving activity if we regard it from outside. Regarded from within, educational activity is entirely a perceiving activity.'

In short: all activities, apart from rhythmic ones, are adverse to health. Everything that is adverse to health has to be counteracted by the higher healing process, through education which is metamorphosed healing. 'The forces inherent in education are metamorphoses of therapeutic forces: They are therapeutic forces transformed. The goal of all our educational thinking must be to transform this thinking so as to rise fruitfully from the level of physical thinking to spiritual thinking.'

Steiner went on to describe a new way of judging that was not based on 'right' and 'wrong' or 'true' and 'false,' but on 'healthy' and 'ill.' This was followed by fundamental considerations regarding the effect of life-infused teaching on the child and the physiology of the will. This latter topic in particular has been worked through in depth over the years and Steiner's indications regarding the will have been fully confirmed by scientific research.

The third lecture concludes with a grim picture: Michael fighting with the dragon while a black veil covers the picture. 'Then one would realize that behind it there is something that must not be shown. …' And the battle with the dragon that must not be shown is the battle with the dragon of the dead, of that which comes from the deadened knowledge of our times. 'There the dragon becomes especially horrible. One might almost say that the correct symbol for institutions of higher education today would be a thick black pall. …'

'To live in the truth means to unite oneself with Michael. We must unite ourselves with Michael whenever we enter the classroom; only through this can we bring with us the necessary strength. Verily, Michael is strong.' The next morning Steiner gave the teachers 'a summary' of what had been said: the second teachers' meditation. Let us summarize again. The fourth and fifth school years were riddled with crises. In the upper school the connection with the students was lost, the teachers could not rise above lecturing and could not find a warm and interested approach to the students. Added to that was the deep lack of trust within the teaching faculty when a small administrative circle was about to be formed. Steiner helped as much as he could. (On average he was with the teachers once a month.) He tried to help with the (interposed) lectures later published as *Deeper Insights into Education* (in: *Balance in Teaching*). The second sentence of the first lecture is: 'After all, the fruitfulness of our activity in an institution like the Waldorf school depends … on the ability of the teachers to develop the attitude that will enable them to carry through their work with assurance and be active in the right way. On this occasion, therefore, I would like to speak in a particular about the teachers themselves.'

Did he ask too much of the teachers? The lectures are not about pedagogical questions but about questions of life style, the overcoming of gymnast, rhetorician and professor who either only act, talk or think. All three have to fuse into one whose actions are imbued with life. The clear division between therapeutic and pedagogical healing touches us. Why? Had it become a habit already to refer what could not be mastered pedagogically to medicine and psychology? The presentations on the physiology of the will relate to the teacher himself as well as to the effect it has on the children when the dual process is developed in the lesson:

> Whenever we guide a child into some form of action while he is thinking, we call forth a state of balance between the formation of carbonic and cyanic acids. In human life everything actually depends upon symmetry being produced between these two things.[16]

The great gestures all express the same: Dear teachers, take hold of these insights, use them to heal yourselves. Become alive and truthful in your doing. Gaining a personal relationship to the teaching content is part of the teacher's self-education. If the subject matter undergoes a certain process in the soul, one inspires creativity of teaching in oneself. It is called the 'immediate source of inspiration' which allows the 'right method to present itself.' This description immediately preceded the veiled battle of Michael with the dragon. It referred to Steiner's words about the sourness of the teacher in the classroom. It seems that these words were called for in October 1923. Steiner's deeply felt pain was noticeable when he spoke of the criminal proceedings against Gandhi; although the British judge admired him greatly personally, he sentenced him to years of imprisonment. Why did Steiner bring this up here? Because it is a picture for the situation where the truth cannot create the right conditions for itself. The truth is that there is a new art of education. Can it create the necessary conditions for itself?[17]

Stage 5

After October 1923 Steiner ceased to give lectures for the teachers only. Between the lectures of October 15 and 16 he also attended a teachers' meeting which was devoted to the written notice given prematurely by a member of the administrative council (a kind of executive board) which had been so difficult to install. An inner opposition had been noticeable when teachers were appointed on 30 March 1923 and was apparent now again. On the outside, people acted according to the agreements, while inwardly rejecting them as well as the school's director, Steiner himself: The general opinion has been that I should select the teachers. We should continue with that, but now the problem is that although that opinion has not changed in fact, it has changed in feeling, in how we look at the situation. I may have to pose the question now of whether the faculty members want to select the teachers themselves.'[18] Steiner called it the 'Stuttgart system.' Many of Steiner's suggestions came up against this kind of opposition, such as his ideas concerning more efficient foreign language teaching or the (initially) failing preparations for the final examination (*Abitur*).

Important indications for the now complete curriculum followed in the fifth and sixth school years. Form and content of the language lessons were revised, but the problems with the students reappeared. The teachers were unable to engage the students in a way that could bring about a fertile pedagogical relationship. The sixth school year brought more failings, which Steiner had to blame on the teachers. In the second but last conference he severely criticized the tiredness of the teachers in class. The 'inner opposition' became apparent in the fact that the lecturing, the academic teaching style, had increased rather than been reduced. The contact with the students was lost. 'I have often mentioned it, but you have not really done much to relieve the situation. ...'[19]

Helplessness speaks out of these words. Again and again he mentioned the lack of interest (in the students) and of enthusiasm for the task in hand. One teacher asked whether the 'Doctor' could not help to establish contact with the pupils. Steiner had to repeat that it was a question of interest, of affinity with the students, of enthusiasm, and not of lectures. We can feel how he came to the conclusion: 'I need to give things a new direction' (July 15, 1924). The last recorded sentence of the last meeting with the teachers on September 3, 1924 is: 'I want to give some lectures later in September or early October about the moral aspects of education and teaching.' It was his last visit to the school.

Stage 6

One often hears this sentence quoted out of context as if it were something that was still objectively missing from Steiner's art of education guidelines. This is not the case. The sentence was spoken in a particular crisis situation at the school and referred to the pedagogical abilities of (mainly) the upper school teachers. 'Moral' means a personal relationship of the teachers towards the students that benefits the latter. Looking at the last meetings we must conclude that the school had not met the expectations of Steiner's new educational paradigm. This comes to expression in a moving way in the farewell letter Steiner wrote to the teachers two weeks before his death.[20] The 'child of concern' to which Steiner had referred at the end of the teacher training course, in the last discussion with the teachers ('For me this Waldorf School will be a veritable child of concern'), was mentioned again in this farewell letter, together with his urgently expressed hope that they should not let go of what they had built up together. If the college of teachers was united by the 'active power of thought' (which was not possible during Steiner's lifetime), it could be done; what had been achieved so far would 'strongly work among the teachers of this school.' 'The Waldorf school is truly a child needing special care, but above all, it is also a visible sign of the fruitfulness of anthroposophy within the spiritual life of mankind.'

> If all teachers faithfully carry within their hearts the awareness of this fruitfulness, the Good Spirits, watching over this school, will be able to work actively; then divine spirit-power will prevail in all the deeds of the teachers.

The 'Stuttgart-miracle' Steiner had to say an outward farewell to the school because he had no 'wings free to fly.' But the school was in a dire situation: it was in danger of losing its identity. The words 'I need to give things a new direction' make sense only in this context.

Despite all these difficulties there were enough people in and around the school who carried within them the living impulse of the art of education. After Steiner's death in March 1925, they were able to work on in his spirit so that the art of education could grow triumphantly all over the world. Not even the atrocities of the Nazi times could stifle this impulse. In Europe, in wide parts of the world, thousands have been inspired by this impulse to develop education out of the art of life. Wherever one is in the world, one has an immediate experience of the healing effect of education if it unites itself with life and allows itself to be nourished by it. If life is understood as the expression of spiritual processes, the art of education can bring about the healing and renewal of our cultural life. We can therefore say that what Steiner very critically referred to as the 'Stuttgart system,' namely the reluctance to comply with his suggestions, was turned into its opposite after his death and became the 'Stuttgart miracle': the educational impulse arose and came to life again.

This paper is also an attempt to show that the problems experienced during the first six years of the Waldorf school are essentially the same we face today, even though the circumstances are different. It also tries to show how Steiner, with his power of judgment, his advice and his unconditional loyalty to the impulse initiated by Emil Molt, tried to help. This can also give direction to us today. All that happened during those six years is archetypal and as valid today as it was then. Maybe it can be seen as a mirror for the school movement today.

ENDNOTES:
1. From Rudolf Steiner's opening address of August 20, 1919, the evening before the teacher training seminar began (first published as *Study of Man*, later as *The Foundations of Human Experience*, CW 293). Also in *Faculty Meetings with Rudolf Steiner* (CW 300a) and *Towards the Deepening of Waldorf Education*, Pedagogical Section.
2. Rudolf Steiner, *The Foundations of Human Experience* (CW 293), Lecture 1, August 21, 1919.
3. Rudolf Steiner, *Discussions with Teachers* (CW 295), Discussion 1, August 21, 1919.
4. Rudolf Steiner, *The Foundations of Human Experience* (CW 293), Lecture 14, September 5, 1919.
5. Rudolf Steiner, *Discussions with Teachers* (CW 295), Third lecture on the curriculum and closing words.
6. Rudolf Steiner, *Balance in Teaching* (CW 302a), Lecture 3, September 21, 1920.
7. Ibid., Lecture 1, September 15, 1920.
8. Rudolf Steiner, *Discussions with Teachers* (CW 295), Closing words to discussion 15, September 6, 1919.
9. See note 7.
10. See note 6.
11. See note 2.
12. Rudolf Steiner, *Education for Adolescents* (CW 301), Lecture 1, 12 June 1921.
13. *Faculty Meetings with Rudolf Steiner* (CW 300b), 20 June 1922.
14. Ibid., 6 February 1923.
15. Rudolf Steiner, *Deeper Insights into Education*. In: *Balance in Teaching* (CW 302a) and the corresponding meeting of October 16, 1923, in *Faculty Meetings with Rudolf Steiner* (CW 300c).
16. Rudolf Steiner, *Balance in Teaching* (CW 302a), Lecture 3.
17. See note 16.
18. *Faculty Meetings with Rudolf Steiner* (CW 300c), March 30, 1923.
19. Ibid., July 15, 1924.
20. In *Towards the Deepening of Waldorf Education*, Pedagogical Section.

A Bold Step Forward

by Andreas Neider
translated by Nina Kuettel

As far as the natural sciences are concerned, Waldorf schools have kept pace. But, often, there is not enough money to make room for modern natural sciences. This was shown to be true at a symposium held at the Freien Waldorfschule in Stuttgart, Germany.

A bold step

The Uhlandshöhe Waldorf School Foundation hosted a public symposium at the beginning of May 2010 in Stuttgart on the topic: *Development of Teaching of the Natural Sciences in Our Schools*. With a prominently occupied podium, the discussion about academic natural sciences was opened.

The Uhlandshöhe Waldorf School Foundation was started in October of 2006, not least of all, to secure the ability of the school to meet the future: a venture that has likely not been seen in the German Waldorf school landscape. The purpose of the foundation is to promote the ability of Waldorf education at the Uhlandshöhe Waldorf School to meet educational needs of the future. The foundation has a special objective with this symposium: to further development the instruction in the natural sciences.

Over and above the financing of regular school operations through parents, donations, and state subsidies, it is important that special projects that are closely associated with the objective of the foundation be promoted. This includes: new and long-term strategies for attracting teachers and aiding young talent, advancing strategies for quality control in instruction, and establishing and managing a natural sciences center for chemistry, physics, and biology.

Certainly, almost all Waldorf schools have a reputation for fine instruction in the arts: good theater, eurythmy, orchestra, and offering interesting learning methods. But what of natural science?

The first Waldorf School in Uhlandshöhe has a special and traditional connection to these disciplines. After the school was founded, Rudolf Steiner held three natural science courses there; the "warmth course," the "light course," and the "astronomy course."

To begin the symposium, biologist Rolf Knippers from the University of Konstanz gave a wide-ranging overview of the state of the sciences in the areas of evolution biology, physics, and astronomy, as well as human medicine and genetics. The audience, made up of parents and teachers from Stuttgart as well as neighboring schools, was immediately absorbed in the subject.

What is needed is also provided by the Waldorf schools.

There followed a lecture by a researcher on electrical current. Christian Liess from the Fachhochschule Konstanz (Technical College) about what today's industries expect from their employees. It may have been a provocative subject for some since Waldorf education sets a completely different course than conforming to the needs of industry. However, among the desired qualities named by Liess were found: a healthy sense of self confidence, creativity, alertness and good judgment, capacity for teamwork, good language skills, and a few other things that are in keeping with the goals of Waldorf education.

In the subsequent discussion, a topic was raised about further desired skills that are much in demand today: fluency in foreign languages, and the ability to think and judge according to scientific criteria, which ability being achieved through education in the natural sciences. Peter Gallin, professor of didactic of mathematics at the University of Zürich, added another focus: Through dialog-based learning, class offerings and their quality would be assessed not only from a teacher's perspective, but also from a student's point of view. There would be reviews to see to what extent an offered class could actually be accepted and processed. For a teacher, this perspective is not always easy considering they are accustomed to lecturing and presenting, but it contributes decisively to the success of their teaching efforts. Like Martin Wagenschein, Gallin is convinced

that real understanding, especially of natural science, is possible only within a dialogue. In this connection, the teacher is less interested in the right answer to a problem being found and much more focused on the path the student has chosen to find the answer. Here also there is strong agreement with a goal of Waldorf education: to bring the students to a sense of independence and autonomy in their learning process.

Experience and mental training in balance

The final talk by Martin Basfeld of the Freie Hochschule für anthroposophische Pädagogik (College of Anthroposophical Education) in Mannheim, Germany, made clear that especially instruction in the natural sciences was in danger of suffocating under the creation of theories. On the other hand, it should not remain in a state of pure phenomenalism. When it comes to instruction in the natural sciences, Waldorf education demands a balance between experience of sense perceptions and training of the mind through theory development.

In the final round of discussion, a practical insight crystallized: Modern instruction in the natural sciences requires appropriately equipped classroom space! What is presently available does not allow classes in natural science to be designed around interesting experiments. What is missing is an open, natural sciences facility that meets the needs of students in a day school with internships available.

For further information please contact

>Stiftung Waldorfschule Uhlandshöhe
>Moerikestrasse 1
>70178 Stuttgart, Germany
>Telephone: 0711-24849794
>Email: stiftung@waldorfschule-uhlandshoehe.de

ÁR VAR ALDA

ÞAT ER YMIR BYGÐI

VARA SANDR NE SÆR

NE SVALAR UNNIR

JORÐ FANNS ÆVA

NE UPHIMMIN

GAP VAR GINNUNGA

EN GRAS HVÆRGI

Internet Crunch

by Mathias Maurer
translated by Nina Kuettel

Just a few years ago these questions were resolved very differently: When does the bus leave? What is that telephone number? – One knew to take a look at the bus schedule or the telephone book and remember the information. Today, nothing functions without the Internet, quick information for a flat rate. Nobody, especially not the user, checks the quality or the validity of this information. It may be right, or, then again, not.

Technology has changed people.

Long ago there was only the spoken word: Stories and reports were spread by word of mouth. Knowledge was imparted by speech. Information was inextricably linked to social events and activities, embedded in human interaction and encounter. Think only of the creation and dissemination of our cultural and spiritual knowledge in the form of myths, epics, legends, fairytales, and religious revelations or cultic practices. They went from mouth to ear. Their authenticity was directly experienced by the listener, through their perception of the speaker.

Then came the written word, and with it the first diminishing of human beings' capacity for memory. Plato proffered this notion already in his "Phaedrus Dialogue": The invention of letters will infuse the mind of the learner with forgetfulness. But through the new technologies for gathering and documenting knowledge and information, unheard of horizons have been opened to us. Modern scientific understanding was born with the printing press. To this day, a printed book represents the validity and reliability of the knowledge and conclusions it contains, regardless of any claims to the contrary. For good reasons the "copy and paste" submissions of students from elementary school to University are not recognized as independent work—if they are noticed. Not simple reproductions, but original and individualized contributions are demanded.

Gerd Gigerenzer, director of The Center of Adaptive Behavior and Cognition at the Max Planck Institute for Education Research in Berlin, asserts that using the Internet changes our thinking because it shifts the search for information from inside our head toward something external. Instead of exerting our long-term memory, we comfortably carry out this search by way of a search engine. That is why many people, especially children, find it difficult to remember fairytales, poems, or songs. Gigerenzer points out another serious difference: In order to glean information from the Net, social skills are no longer required. His conjectures appear to be confirmed by Gary Small, professor of psychiatry at the University of California in Los Angeles. Neuropsychology has established that our thinking has changed as a result of the Internet, smart phones, and the like. Constant access to multimedia changes not only the activity patterns in our brain, but also our learning and social behavior. Thus, Internet use influences and structures areas of the brain that are responsible for how we solve problems, recognize and control emotions, concentrate, and our ability to postpone immediate desires for the sake of long-term goals. A study conducted with eight- to twenty-three-year-olds showed that they misinterpret emotional signals, and that face to face communication is difficult for them. The biological memory becomes weaker if we no longer memorize things, but instead only learn where we can find the information the quickest.

> *Definitions* strain the memory
> *The vividly artistic* cultivate the memory
> *Efforts of will* fortify the memory.
> – Rudolf Steiner

In the *Frankfurter Allgemeinen Zeitung* (newspaper), the neuroscientist and learning researcher, Manfred Spitzer formulated it briefly and drastically: The constant use of media makes us not only dense but also dull. Content and substance are absolutely no longer mentally processed, and when violent acts occur, instead of stepping in to help, out comes the mobile phone, and the video is uploaded on the Internet.

There are many kinds of memory.

Katherine Nelson, a developmental psychologist in New York, describes the memory as a bio-socio-cultural system.. The following distinct memory forms are direct catalysts to a person's sense of identity:

- There is the *social memory* that is strongly permeated with familial ties. Just how strongly can be seen by the example of the honor killing of Hatun Sueruecue in Berlin, the purpose of which was to restore the identity of a social cohesion – the family honor.

- There is the *cultural memory*, into which everything flows that embeds us within a national or ethnic context. Without a valid passport at every border crossing, one is virtually without identity. In his novel *Stiller*, Max Frisch plausibly depicts the problems that can occur if this classification system does not function.

- Finally, there is *communicative memory* that is applied especially through language. Harald Welzer, director of the Kulturwissenschaftlichen Institut (Cultural Science Institute) in Essen, and psychologist Hans-Joachim Markowitsch in Bielefeld, assert that increased language competency and memory development virtually form a single unit, and that not only the content, but also the structure of memory is formed through spoken communication.

According to Colin Trevarthen, human infancy researcher at the University of Edinburgh, up to age two the memory is working almost completely as "body-implicit." Thus, small children do not yet have an autobiographical memory. The child first differentiates and integrates the various levels of memory with the ability to speak.

One thing is clear: Facilitating good speech and differentiated verbal expression practiced through compassionate, empathic, and emotion-supported dialogues—so-called memory talks—leads to firm support for the memory. This socio-cultural aspect is in turn tied in with certain phases of brain development that are completed only after puberty.

The anthroposophical view on memory

In his book *The Study of Man*, Rudolf Steiner went much further than a bio-socio-cultural frame of reference. For him, memory was not to be found in the head. He compared remembering with awaking, and forgetfulness with a process of going to sleep. When we remember something, we do not call forth warehoused notions from some area of the brain; we newly perceive what has been literally embodied in us as a memory. The storage facility for these images was described by Steiner as the etheric body, the carrier of all life and formative processes in our body. What is remembered is not the substance of perceptions or ideas but the mental, pictorial experiences associated with them: feeling impulses, tensions, or moods that have been written into this "body." And there is more: Polar to the process of remembering, the experience impresses its form even into our physical organs and shapes our way of remembering.

Ernst-Michael Kranich, anthropologist and Waldorf educator, elaborated on the importance of the connection between activities and development of the capacity for remembering. In this respect it is obvious that one speaks of a physically connected memory that is supported by the whole body. The contents of this memory are brought forth again by way of feelings and the will, not by way of the intellect through the use of memory exercises.

Steiner formulated his teaching on memory like this: "Definitions strain the memory. The vividly artistic cultivates the memory. Efforts of will—activities of will—fortify the memory." Looked at in this way, the Internet represents an assault on the autonomous life of our feeling and willing natures because they unfold in time and space. The Internet user is relieved of any effort: He wants and gets the result immediately.

The abolishment of memory and its consequences

According to Aleida Assmann, literature scientist at the University of Konstanz, the increasing transference of knowledge onto the Internet represents a massive process of dematerialization. But our memory requires the material, or human, preservation of knowledge because the Internet, in its basic structure, is not very reliable or stable, and is, basically, a memory without support, that networks, extracts, and assesses. Cultural and social memories and the individual memories associated with them (autobiographical memory) are altered depending upon which medium is used to convey knowledge and information. This applies especially when the remembering itself (Facebook, Youtube, etc. are examples) becomes a media event of self-production. Goetz Grossklaus, a media historian in Karlsruhe, emphasized how the flood of images in the form of photos, videos, films, and computer animations represents an important creative component of the Internet – more than the mediums of speech and writing – that stands in close proximity to our internal images that are connected to our remembering and our imagination.

The craving of images is something that is inborn in human beings. It is the yearning of the soul for inner movement. We live in a time when the creation of an internal treasury of images is made more difficult because we receive images only from the outside. The more the internal world of images is impoverished, the more hunger there is for external images. External images only appear to feed the soul. Externalization empties the soul more and more. They distort and falsify the image we have of ourselves and others. World-image and self-image are composed of countless splinters of images that do not follow any internal connection. In their omnipresence they threaten to cover up the internal world of images and the "true" self. Even today, Native Americans shy away from being photographed because they believe the photos "catch" their soul. Photographs highlight a fleeting present moment in the totality that knows no past and no future. When looking at a photograph, who has not said: "That's not me, is it?" The human ego, or "I," checks to see if the souvenir picture is identical to the actual event, or perceived object or self image, or if it is just an illusion. It looks past the picture to what is remembered.

Roy Baumeister, social psychologist at Florida State University, speaks of "ego exhaustion": The human will is paralyzed when, through a flood of information and images, it must permanently decide what is important or not. The energy to concentrate and actively limit can no longer be summoned.

All of the memory content is externalized. The person appears as a being who is devoid of memory and whose mind is increasingly "removed." And the question arises as to whether a person without memory, without a history of their internal world, even loses their "I"? This scenario became famous through the Stanley Kubrick film based on the science fiction novel *A Clockwork Orange* by Anthony Burgess. In one scene, Alex, the main character, has his eyelids held open and is forced to view violent images over and over. What was thought to be re-socialization therapy is actually the same as tortuous brainwashing. The protagonist becomes an egoless, hollow form, with catastrophic results.

The Italian sociologist Elena Esposito would probably agree with Plato's fear quoted at the beginning of this article because, for her, modern communication media are "tools of forgetfulness." Otherwise the overabundance of information simply could not be dealt with. Thus, storing information is not remembering information, and most certainly not communicative usage. Esposito even proclaimed the "telematic revolution" whereby the technology user, sucked into electronic mediums, virtually melts into them and is carried along on the never dwindling stream of data. Subject and object become one. Whether the evidence she offers of stronger interest in religious and esoteric subjects is actually heralding a countermovement, and giving back some orientation to the "digital natives," is questionable. A one-dimensional world is always a pitfall for the "I."

www.ingramcontent.com/pod-product-compliance
Lightning Source LLC
Chambersburg PA
CBHW041525220426
43670CB00002B/32